SURVIVING THE UNTHINKABLE
A Memoir Of Resilience And Hope

Martin Gomez

Dedication

To My Lord and Savior, Jesus,

Lord of Lords, King of Kings,

Thank you so much for helping me endure all trials and tribulations.

It is in His name that I also dedicate this to my mother and mother-in-law, Enedina Estrada, and my second mom, Pola Garcia, who went to see Jesus today, August 17, 2024. I will miss her dearly. Today, while at her hospital bedside with Johnny, his older son, and me, as we prayed by her side, she got up and back to the bed. With all the tubes in her mouth and eyes closed. Holy Spirit came upon me stronger than Johnny felt. It almost knocked me to the floor. I confirmed this with my pastor. I asked him why I felt it so strongly while Johnny and Gus didn't, and he told me that I experienced it with greater intensity. Once again, the Holy Spirit came upon me, this time with power. I had never felt that before. Now I understand why the Bible says that no man can withstand His presence; if it comes upon you at full strength, you will perish, as God's Word says.

To me and John.

Christopher— my nephew. This is how GOD gave me the feeling of what being a DAD feels like.

Acknowledgments

I would like to express my heartfelt gratitude to the following individuals who have supported and guided me throughout the creation of this book:

Enedina Estrada for her valuable input and encouragement.

My mom for her constant love and support.

Johnny Garcia for his unwavering assistance.

Blanca Dora Frias, thank you for your encouragement and help.

Sergio Frias for his support and guidance.

Javier, my brother, for his understanding and help.

My pastor, Macario Segura, for his spiritual guidance.

Leobis Segura, the pastor's wife, for her support and encouragement.

My Lord and Savior, Jesus Christ, for His divine inspiration and strength.

I am deeply grateful to each of you for your contributions to this work.

Amen.

Contents

Dedication...i

Acknowledgments iii

Chapter 1: The Beginning.. 1

Chapter 2: Shoe Shining.. 8

Chapter 3: The Abuse 15

Chapter 4: Drugs.. 29

Chapter 5: Prison 37

Chapter 6: Safeway House.. 44

Chapter 7: Love 50

Chapter 8: Ambulance Incident 54

Chapter 9: The Accident.. 63

Chapter 10: The Tumor 71

Chapter 11: The Aftermath 77

Chapter 12: My Mother 84

Chapter 13: Today and Tomorrow 91

Final Reflection 97

Chapter 1: The Beginning

My journey began in the scorching heat of Mexicali, Baja California. I was born into a world of challenges. I defied the odds from the very beginning. With its heated sun and unforgiving terrain, Mexicali echoed the struggles I would face throughout my life. I gaudily recall one incident from my early childhood. It was a memory etched in my mind like a scar on the desert landscape. I found myself stuck in the middle of scorching sand, my feet burning beneath me. I was lost in the hunt for food since I was very hungry as I walked too far from safety and my mother's reach.

When I got lost, I stood there, paralyzed by fear. Meanwhile, my mother was panicky and searching for me. But that wasn't the only encounter with death I experienced in my youth. I can count at least seven times when my life hung in the balance—each instance a proof of my resilience and the protective hand of fate. That was the first time I encountered danger in my life.

One particularly disturbing memory stands out. The day I fell into a dry well. As darkness enveloped me, I could hear the desperate cries of my family searching above. I was alone in the depths, crying. I clung to hope, whereas my heart was pounding with the uncertainty of my fate.

Then there was the incident at Eagle Town Park, marked by an act of cruelty that I couldn't forget. There was an incident at Eagle Lake. It was a charter park with a swimming pool. One moment, I was enjoying the simple pleasures of childhood. The very next day, I was thrust into the depths of a pool. I remember how difficult it was for me. My godfather took me there and just threw me there. I was trying hard to gasp for air as the water overwhelmed me. In that moment of terror, I questioned the motives of those around me. Was it a prank gone wrong or something more sinister? I was confused as to why such a thing happened to me.

As I arose from the water, badly coughing and perplexed, I searched for answers that remained intangible. Moreover, my family's absence during this suffering added to the confusion, and their presence on the other side of the border was a blunt reminder of the distance between us. As I look back, I realize that these early trials helped me shape the person I would become. Undoubtedly, I have become a survivor and quite tough in the face of danger. Mexicali may have been the birthplace of my challenges, but it was also the crucible in which my strength was forged.

Growing up, life was full of rapid experiences—both joyful and sorrowful. Most of my childhood memories were etched in the bustling town where life unfolded against the backdrop of Mexicali's dusty streets. Although I have no memories of my time in Mexicali, Baja, California, it became the backdrop for the childhood adventures that shaped my early years. The images of that place have become indelibly linked to the stories of my youth, even if the details themselves remain fuzzy. Among the several challenges of directing a new country and culture, a figure stood out as an example of stability in my young life. It was none other than my stepfather. He was more than just a guardian. He stood as a strong supporter and was an embodiment of fatherhood. He was a constant source of love and guidance in my life, which was full of challenges. I cherish the memories of our outings together and the simple pleasures of sipping coffee and indulging in sweets. I reminisced as his hand warmed in mine as we explored the world around us. But life doesn't stay the same and is not without its struggles.

Financial hardships appeared large during that time, forming a shadow over our finite moments of happiness. My father, being courageous despite the difficulties, remained a steadfast presence. He was a pillar of strength in a world troubled by uncertainty. I never knew that this strength would be taken away from me. Tragically, the only stability I had come to rely on was shattered by the sudden loss of my stepfather. His passing rushed our family into chaos. It left behind a void that could never be filled. He had been more than just a provider. He was my confidant, my mentor, and my rock.

In the midst of grief, memories of our time together became bittersweet treasures. I used to cherish remnants of a past era. I recall the day he gifted me a watch that was a token of his affection, and I traded it for a tarp—a decision made in innocence yet loaded with significance. It was a symbol of the carefree days of childhood that always brought joy. It was a time before the weight of responsibility bore down on me. Fortunately, despite the hardships, there were moments of joy and friendship. I fondly remember playing marbles with friends. It was the thrill of competition and the camaraderie of shared laughter. In those momentary but beautiful moments, the cares of the world melted away and were replaced by the simple joys of youth. Life seemed to get better with time, but the very next moment, tragedy struck once more. I usually take a routine trip to the store with my sister, but this time, it ended in disaster. A speeding car sped into us and shattered the illusion of safety. Miraculously, we survived, but the confrontation with death left a permanent mark on my psyche. For me, it was a reminder of life's fragility and the importance of seizing each moment with gratitude.

As I reflect on my childhood, I am reminded of the resilience that lies within us all, a strength forged in the crucible of adversity. Mexicali may have been a town of trials, but it was also a place of resilience, where bonds were forged in the fires of hardship.

Life becomes much easier if your parents stand with you at each step. My parents, Jose Gomez, were my real father, and my mother was Enedina Estrada. My stepdad, Julian, was an inspiration and light in my life. He'd wake me up in the mornings to share coffee and bread before we began our day. His presence was the anchor I needed, especially since we had faced tragedies back-to-back—losing a sister and then him. The pain was unbearable. Life didn't remain the same after his passing. Without Dad, life felt like a turbulent sea that tossed me between grief and survival. I found myself back on the streets, shining shoes to make ends meet. But even before that, I had crossed borders, seeking comfort from my aunt and godfather. Little did I know that the very person meant to protect me—my uncle—would shatter my innocence at such a tender age. It was the most difficult phase of my life.

I was brutally sexually abused by my uncle. One day, we were eating supper, and he said, Go and wash your hands. So he took me, pulled his pants down, and made me do oral sex. My legs were shaking, and my calves were shaking, scared. Then he would raped me. I was so scared. I didn't know what to do or whom to tell. The trauma of abuse silenced me in a way that, though I wanted so hard to scream and yell, I didn't do anything. I trapped my anguish within. I never told anyone about it. Even after my uncle's demise, the scars remained and haunted me. I found myself knotted up with gangs, seeking protection in their brotherhood. But the violence and chaos only deepened my despair.

One night, the streets turned into a battleground. It echoed with the clash of rival gangs. Fear gripped me as I found myself caught in the crossfire, narrowly escaping with my life. But in the aftermath, there was an emptiness inside me that grew deeper, and I turned to drugs for escape. The grip of addiction tightened with time. It suffocated me with each passing day. The weight of my past and the struggles of the present bore down on me like a persistent storm that pushed me to the edge. Among the weight of my past, there was this terrible memory that imprinted on my mind. I could never forget how my father's anger erupted into violence and how brutally he began to strike my mother. It was traumatizing for me, being a child, to witness that cruelty. But one day, my mom gathered courage and stood against my dad. Her cries for help echoed through the walls of our home, which was supposed to be a secure place for us. It was a haunting melody of fear and desperation. It was a nightmare that seemed to have no end. In a moment of bravery, she called my grandpa for help. With a heavy heart, he intervened. He rescued us from the clutches of fear and turmoil and took us away from there. We moved to El Monte, Maulipas, to start over. It was a scary time, but also a fresh start for us away from the bad stuff. Under the shelter of his protective arms, we found refuge and a glimmer of hope. Hence, together, we embarked on a journey to a new beginning. We left behind the scars of the past as we set course for El Monte Maulipas. Fortunately, it was a bittersweet escape, as it was filled with both relief and uncertainty. Yet, in the embrace of our new surroundings, we dared dream of a life free from the shadows of violence.

I remember when we used to go out to the country to pick cotton. I remember helping my mom with it where my grandfather and grandmother lived. My grandpa fought alongside the soldiers against Pancho Villa, perhaps because they offered better pay for a chance at a slightly better life. After retiring from his service, the government rewarded him with a small piece of land. It must have been a significant journey for him, from the battlefield to the peaceful ownership of land. The land dedicated to my grandpa was about half an acre, and he always said it would be mine one day. But after he passed away, my grandma ended up selling it.

While I was out shoe-shining, my grandmother took care of me, along with my two sisters and brother. My mother was across the border in the USA, working hard to pick tomatoes, cucumbers, onions, oranges, grapefruits, and more. She would send money to my grandma to ensure we had enough to eat.

I used to leave home early in the morning to shoe shine and come back in the evening. I would buy day-old bread with the little change that I made during the whole day of shoe-shining. While I was helping out with Shine, I was just trying to make ends meet, and when we went back to living in the mountains, where we used to have fun, we'd go to Rio Grande and do some border mapping with our slippers. We'd also make and sell candies sometimes. My stepdad was really good at making them. He was a nice person, and I have fond memories of him. But one day, he suddenly got sick. My mom rushed him to the hospital, but he passed away on the way there. It was a really tough time for us, especially since we had already gone through losing a sister before that. My stepdad used to be the best part of my days, especially when he'd wake me up in the mornings to share coffee and bread before we started our day. Losing him was another big blow.

Chapter 2: Shoe Shining

There is a sweet memory that I hold close to my heart—the recollection of the moment when my mom met my stepdad. It was a beautiful beginning, setting the stage for the sweet journey ahead. It was the most precious time when they two met. It all started in the cozy kitchen. The kitchen atmosphere was filled with the warmth of a butane burner and was full of stuff as they were making candies with milk. This vinyl-topped desk was where my mom and stepdad concocted their delicious treats and became the center of our bustling household.

In that kitchen, the galvanized tub was reminiscent of simpler times—the simple yet precious time when they mixed ingredients like jam and sugar to create their signature delights. It was the most joyful sight to watch and enjoy. Like a conductor guiding an orchestra, my stepdad would expertly exert a metal hook to fill the yams with sweetness while I eagerly assisted. I always loved learning the art of candy-making by his side.

There were so many beautiful events that occurred, and I have always cherished my memories. As I reflect on the events leading up to his untimely death, the kitchen takes on a bittersweet description. Yet, amidst the sorrow, there is resilience. My mother and I find ourselves in a new place, where I take up the role of a shoe-shiner. It was a demonstration of our persistent determination to forge ahead despite life's challenges. Life continued its way by sending various hardships our way. But those candies became an encouragement to hope, reminding me of the strength and unity of our family. Just as each candy was meticulously crafted with love and care, so too were the bonds that held us together. The candies themselves were a witness to our ingenuity and resourcefulness.

Crafted from simple ingredients like peanuts and milk, they were filled with a richness that exceeded their humble origins. Whether it was the creamy texture of the milk candies or the peanut brittle crunch, each confection carried a piece of our story.

At that time, I spent time selling those treats on street corners, and it filled me with both pride and nostalgia. Those candies were not just supplies to be bought and sold; they were tangible expressions of our family's love and resilience, shared with the world one sweet bite at a time. Just as the candies varied in shape and flavor, so too did our experiences. Yet, through it all, we remained united, drawing strength from each other and the memories we had created together.

It wasn't just about the candies themselves; it was about the moments shared and the bonds forged in the process. Some memories of that time we spent together were the candies we once made; our family was a blend of different flavors and textures. It was so wonderful coming together to create something truly special. My parents were hard workers, and my stepdad was also a tailor. Apart from that, my stepfather always took special care of my mother. My dad did not let her wash clothes because she was pregnant with my sister. So she had a lady who used to wash our clothes. So, though life may have its ups and downs, the memories we shared in that kitchen will always remain a source of sweetness in my heart. Soon, the happiness in our lives took a turn and spread out, with the weight of grief and loss pressing heavily upon our hearts. Three months prior, my stepdad Julian's passing had left a void in our lives. I was devastated and in utter shock. The void got deeper when combined with the departure of my sister. I couldn't believe what I saw with my eyes. My little sister lay peacefully, her tiny form adorned like a princess—a cotton crown resting upon her head. Her departure shook me to the core, leaving me grappling with questions of faith and fate as I questioned God about why he did this to me and my mom.

Julian, my stepdad, followed shortly after my little sister. The world seemed to tilt on its axis. I will never forget the terrible sight of him lying motionless in the casket, which shocked me to the core and filled me with disbelief and complete denial. I was in shock and in denial mode, as I wasn't ready to accept the fact that he was no longer with us. Was he truly gone or merely sleeping? I struggled to comprehend the finality of death. I was yearning for him to awaken and dismiss the terrifying sight and reality that had enveloped us.

As I recalled that time of my childhood, I couldn't help but notice the impact that family dynamics and personal beliefs had on our lives. My mother's strong faith in the power of dreams and superstitions passed down from her grandfather and shaped our understanding of the world around us. When my dad told Mom about his dream of flowers with my little sister, I couldn't help but think of all the other times dreams have come true for us. I vividly remember when my stepfather had a dream involving a flower gathering, believing it was a sign from beyond. Days later, he passed away. This experience set my mother's belief in the significance of dreams and their ability to offer indications into the future. My own experiences with dreams and superstitions further strengthened this belief. I've always been fascinated by the patterns and symbols that appear in my dreams, often finding connections between them and events in my life.

For example, I've noticed that dreaming of poop usually precedes financial gains. White water means sickness. If I hit my right elbow by mistake, it's an argument. If I itch on my right hand, then it means that money will come, but you have to hit it in the palm 5 times so it comes true. Money usually precedes financial gains, while dreaming of dirty water can foretell gossip or trouble. If you dream a lot of money, then it's usually the opposite. It means that you going to be poor. One particular superstition that has stuck with me is the belief that cutting your toenails or fingernails with scissors can lead to a death in the family. I've always been mindful of this superstition and have avoided cutting my nails with scissors. Another superstition I've encountered involves walking inside with an open umbrella. It's believed to bring bad luck. I've always made sure to close my umbrella before entering a building. While some may dismiss these beliefs as superstitions, I've personally experienced their strange accuracy. These experiences have deepened my connection to the unseen forces that shape our lives.

After losing two of my beloved family members, I felt lifeless. My whole existence felt like a burden to my soul. Life was no longer the same, and nothing excited me the way I used to. Depression settled over me like a suffocating blanket. It became a relentless companion in the wake of so much loss. I questioned the future, unsure of where life would lead us next. Fear and uncertainty troubled me on the inside. There was a constant reminder of my weakness in a world suddenly devoid of familiar and supportive anchors.

Yet, amidst the darkness, a glimmer of hope emerged. My grandparents became silent pillars of strength. They wholeheartedly offered sanctuary and stability to me and my family. It was their firm presence that became a hope of reassurance in turbulent times. It was due to my grandmother's care that my siblings found comfort, while I sought shelter in the streets to earn a meager living selling popsicles and chiclets. The streets became my classroom. The streets and situations that occurred taught me so many things after my stepdad's demise. They taught me the value of flexibility and hard work in the face of hardship. Each step that I took was a demonstration of my determination to survive for my family. I remained like a rock for my family even as my feet bore the scars of countless journeys over the challenging roadway. I spent my days on the streets, pushing my cart through the bustling streets. I became a silent witness to the ebb and flow of life. I was never ashamed of my situation. I courageously faced struggles and mirrored them in the faces of those around me. Like a river flowing inevitably toward an uncertain horizon, I directed the currents of loss and longing, guided by the memory of those I had loved and lost.

In the end, the bounciness and strength of the human spirit succeeded. I overcame the hardships, though the shadows of loss may remain. After the deaths of my stepdad and sister, we relocated to Reynosa, a bustling border town teeming with opportunity and uncertainty. It settled on the banks of the Rio Grande. Reynosa gestures with promises of a fresh start, even as the shadows of loss remain in our hearts.

For me, the transition to Reynosa marked a shift from selling popsicles to shining shoes. This humble occupation became a lifeline in our new surroundings. The dirty streets became my field, where each shoe was polished to a glossy shine. Among the hustle and bustle of the border town, the sweet and bitter memories of Rio Bravo remain like echoes of a distant past. In Reynosa, the beat of life pulses with an energy all its own. It was the border serving as a connection where cultures collide and dreams take flight. Yet beneath the surface lies an intense tension. It was a reminder of the unwarranted balance between hope and despair that defines life on the edge of the border. Fortunately, in the face of difficulty, Reynosa becomes an encouragement to hope. It was a place where new beginnings were born from the ashes of the past. Though the road ahead may be tense with challenges, I am sustained by the knowledge that I am not alone and that, with each step forward, I carry with me the love and support of those who have gone before.

Now, while looking back at my journey, I am filled with a sense of gratitude for the infinite opportunities that lie ahead. Even as I carry the weight of loss in my heart, Reynosa may be a new chapter in my story, but the bonds of family and love that bond us remain firm. It guided me through the trials and successes that lie ahead.

Chapter 3: The Abuse

Abuse is a terrible, dark shadow that can cast itself over every feature of a person's life. It leaves the person confused with multiple scars that may never fully heal. Abuse damages not just the body but also the soul of a person, whether the abuse is physical, emotional, or psychological. Abuse takes many forms and can occur in various situations, from intimate relationships to domestic environments. Its deceptive nature often blooms in silence while leaving victims feeling isolated and powerless. Yet, by shedding light on this inescapable issue, we can begin to break the chains of silence and stigma. By creating awareness, we can offer hope and support to those who have endured its torment. My life also depicts the torment that I have endured since the early years of my life.

I remember heading home one day. I was six years old, and I unexpectedly found myself stepping onto something unusual. It was a dry well that scared the shit out of me. However, this wasn't just any ordinary well; it was covered with a thin layer of galvanized material, making it quite fragile. It looks like the type of material that is often used for roofing, but in this case, it covered the opening of the well. It was an easily breakable thing.

When I stepped onto that, I gingerly balanced myself on the dangerous surface as soon as I realized the potential danger beneath my feet. The sight of someone accidentally breaking through and dropping into the depths below sent a shiver down my spine. It was an odd and unexpected obstacle on my journey home. It was not the first time that I encountered danger and got stuck in something dangerous. Previously, I had fallen in the swimming pool. After going through such repeated instances of abuse, I found myself longing for safety and security. Yet, each time I required safety, I encountered only more trauma. After that incident, I got so terrified that I returned home, shaken by the terror of yet another violation.

It was the third time I had experienced such horror, and the trauma hung heavy on my fragile and young shoulders. But that wasn't just my fate; it had another cruel twist in store for me. I recall a morning when I woke up to find my aunt and my godfather visiting our home. They often came to our home and brought supplies to my grandfather, including bugler cigarettes and tobacco. These were the items that he cherished dearly. My aunt would thoroughly prepare these gifts for us, ensuring they were ready for the journey. I remember the different smells of tobacco lasting in the air as they entered our home—bearing several gifts, including a toy truck for me. Despite the gestures of kindness, there was an underlying tension that I couldn't comprehend. It was a silent understanding of the darkness that waited beneath the surface.

While everyone was sitting and chatting happily, the conversation soon turned to the topic of bringing me to the United States. I wouldn't deny that part of me desired the opportunity to escape the horrors of my reality. In contrast, another part of me stuck desperately to the safety of my mother's grip since I was just a six-year-old and was attached to my mom. I had a fear of leaving behind my mother in Mexico.

The abuse started when I moved to the U.S. at my aunt's house. I was around seven years old. There were many people in the house, like my aunt, uncle, and six children—three girls and three boys. So one fine day, we were eating supper, and he said, "Go and wash your hands." Everybody was at the table, but he accompanied me discreetly to the washroom. So, he took me, pulled his pants down, and made me do oral sex. I was traumatized. My legs were shaking, and my calves were shaking, scared. Then he would rape me. I was so scared. I didn't know what to do or whom to tell. I was completely traumatized and unable to understand what had just happened. Then he left the washroom.

I never told anyone about it since I had nobody by my side to disclose that my uncle molested me. I wanted to tell my aunt, but I never did; my mom wasn't there with me. I remember that all I wanted was to go back home. I wanted to go back to my mom. I was alone there among so many people. My sister was with my grandma, so I was the only one from my family there. I was deeply affected by what happened.

At such an early age, I endured so much. I experienced both heartbreak and trauma. I felt scared and alone in the U.S. with nobody to protect, which was incredibly difficult. I desperately wanted to be with my mom, where I felt safe in her arms and comfortable in her hug. The next time my uncle tried to kill me was when I went to school and took a trip to Mexico. Before that, something significant happened. My godfather, who was supposed to be my protector, threw me into the swimming pool. I remember it being a circular pool. Suddenly, I found myself submerged in the water. I still get anxious when I recall that time. I struggled so hard to stay afloat. It was terrifying—I felt like I was drowning and would die. The water was deep, over my head. It was about five feet. I recall it intensely—it was a close call. I was struggling to stay afloat, but somehow, I managed to swim to the side of the pool and pull myself out. Weirdly, there wasn't anyone else around when it happened.

There were just me, him, and some strangers that I didn't know. It seemed like he secured it right after throwing me in. I didn't see any of my cousins or familiar faces nearby. Thankfully, I was saved. It felt like my uncle was trying to silence me, fearing I might tell someone what happened and he'd face consequences. He had a history of abusing my aunt right from the start. There were times he'd hit her, and she endured a lot because of him. So, when he threw me into the pool, it was like they were both scared—I could tell my aunt was terrified. I knew I couldn't say anything because she might have faced even more harm. It was a tough situation all around.

Then I decided to go back to Mexico. I missed my mother and siblings; therefore, I went back to my home. The journey from Mexico to the U.S. was relatively easy back then. Back then, crossing the border wasn't as strict as it is now. They had papers for their sons; I was included under that guise. Being young and knowing a bit of English worked in my favor, as immigration didn't ask too many questions. However, when I returned later, things had changed. By then, I was doing odd jobs like shoe-shining to get by.

In 1979, when I made the trip back, I was a bit older. This time, I carried a pillow with me, perhaps as a small comfort during the journey. They had a truck with a camper attached—a trailer where my cousins slept in the back on a bed. I remember lying down and acting as a makeshift pillow while they rested their heads on me during the journey back to the States in 1979. That was the last time I went back to Mexico. I stayed in the States after that. Both of us, my mom and I, made the decision to move to the U.S.A. due to the financial poverty and ongoing struggles that we faced in Mexico. Though it wasn't an easy decision to move, it was necessary for a better future. My mom knew that staying where we were wasn't maintainable, and we wanted to give ourselves an opportunity for a much better life. We knew that if we stayed there longer, we'd continue struggling. My mom wanted to ensure that not just me but everyone in the family had the opportunity for a safe and brighter future. She made the journey first, and I followed later, leaving my grandma, sisters, and brother behind.

At that time, the plan was for all of us to move to the U.S. My mom was employed at a cabinetry company called Lido's Cabinetry in East Bernard, Texas. She diligently saved money and arranged for us to join her. However, my aunt and godfather charged my mom for their help in making the arrangements. So, the idea was for my friend, my grandma, and me to join my mom in the U.S. My grandma was able to obtain a passport because of her age and her marriage to a U.S. citizen, who happened to be my godfather. It was understood that everyone in the family would eventually migrate to the U.S., so it was okay for me to return again. We followed through with the plan, but even to this day, nobody knew the full extent of what had happened to me.

This molestation continued and happened to me several times, and not just once. I went back and forth, and it happened again every time I returned to the U.S. On one of those occasions, when I crossed paths with my uncle, he gave me a silver dollar and told me that I could buy whatever I wanted with it. So, I did just that, and then he took me to meet some of their relatives. They had a cornfield there, and I went to visit it with them. I was tired of facing difficult circumstances in Mexico and wanted to escape the suffering that I was experiencing. Coming to the United States seemed like a way to end that suffering and be reunited with your mom, who was already here.

Unfortunately, he kept on molesting me, even in Eagle Lake. My aunt knew that he was abusing me. Significant events happened during that time in my life when I was around fourteen or fifteen years old. I made the journey to the U.S. for the second time, and it seemed like an interesting experience, but I somehow managed to cross it. When I was around fourteen years old, I made the journey to the U.S. for the second time. This experience, although challenging, seemed relatively manageable for me at that age. However, it's disheartening to hear that the person responsible for my past trauma is still engaging in harmful behavior.

Moving forward, I was in my early twenties when this person passed away. During this time, I was balancing work and continuing my education, having completed grades six through nine. My connection to Rosenburg has remained reliable throughout these years, almost like a familiar landmark guiding my journey. Amidst my academic pursuits, you found solace in dance, a form of expression that allowed you to escape and find joy. The dance hall became a sanctuary where I could lose myself in the beat and movement.

So, when I was shoe-shining in Mexico, I lived with my cousins and would shoe-shine with them. One of them was my favorite cousin, and we used to hang around all the time. I always went out shoe-shining with him. On the other hand, my mom wasn't always the best at picking boyfriends. For her, looks seemed to matter more than a good job or how they treated us. It was like she kept chasing after these cute young guys who wouldn't give us a stable life. I was in 9th grade at the time.

One time, she met this guy from Mexico before I was even born. Years later, he started parading around with another woman right in front of our house. He split with

Mom, leaving her nine months pregnant. Mom got jealous and maybe wanted to escape the situation, so she completely ignored our warnings. We pleaded with her not to take us to Mexico so that it would mess up our lives. But she never listened to us. Never. Everyone told Mom going back to Mexico to have the baby was a bad idea, but hey, listening wasn't her strong suit.

So, she packed us up and headed south to where her family lived. It was the same place she took me as a baby. We stayed there for a while before coming back to the border town of Nuevo Progreso. It was a town where they would play music outside the movie theater all day. There were various shops for tourists around the border, and there was a clothing store where my sister, who was still struggling, found her first job. Also, crossing the border wasn't easy. It involved a bus ride all the way to Reynosa, Mexico, and then on to the border town of McAllen in Hidalgo County, Texas. My destination was the Manhattan gas station, which was located in Hidalgo.

Then came the crazy part, which was getting my mom and brothers back. We found them in a tiny house. Apparently, they killed a pigeon, and they were going to eat some pigeons. Desperate, I used my cousin's baptism certificate to cross back into the U.S. and get work. There was a guy who'd gather people waiting for odd jobs— unloading trucks, hauling potatoes, peppers, onions, the whole lot. I'd get paid and come back to Mexico with the money, and that's how we survived for a month or two.

Finally, it was time to bring them back for good. This time, everyone had fake IDs—my little cousin even lent me his birth certificate for his baby sister. Sneaking them across wasn't easy, but I did it. Three trips in total were a crazy experience for them, but I managed. It wasn't easy, but I could work, and they'd wait for me at the bus stop, listening for the familiar sound.

Looking back, it all stemmed from a responsibility I felt after my grandpa and stepdad passed away. They told me I was the man of the house, with two little ones to take care of. That's the story of how my brother ended up back in Mexico.

We went to Rio Grande, La Posta, and that's when I had dreams. Now, what I want to specify about that dream is that it looks like the devil wants to silence me, even if I can't talk and I can't move. I was paralyzed. That's kind of like a primitive idea that I was going to be raped and stuff. I wasn't able to say anything to anybody, you know. Maybe the Lord was trying to tell me something, or the enemy was doing it because that was going to happen to me. When I was going through all these times when I almost passed away and stuff, God was there with me. So that dream even says it all, because I held on to the Lord and believed in Him.

This dream started coming when I was a little kid, and my grandma and grandpa had a little land space. We used one room for the kitchen and the other to sleep. People would say that there were witches at night. It was a ranch called La Posta, which means the post. I was 4 or 5 years old. I would go to sleep, and I would feel something evil. We didn't have light there, as there was no electricity. We would use those oil lamps at night. There were almost 150 people on that Ranch. So when I would go to sleep, I would feel that someone had put their hands on my mouth. So I would not scream, and I couldn't move either until I started to pray to My Father, who is in heaven, holy. Be thy name in the kingdom come, thy will be done. One day, my cousin woke us up because there was a snake inside the room. It was on the roof. It was a big, ol' snake. We're used to living in that place. It was in the back of the yard. It was like a barranca. It was funny. So, he saw the snake and woke us all up. I don't know if it was poisonous or not. It was big. Anyhow, I never saw it completely because it was at night. At night, there were also big ol' birds. They would whistle every time they passed by. There were rumors that they would get the babies and shut their belly buttons out or something.

I'll say the prayer, and then I wake up and pray. It was evil; there was something evil. At that time, I was a child and close to God, and God helps me with these evil deeds—it's a good thing. So God has been helping me since I was a small child. God knew that I was going to go to the church, and the devil knew that too. So that's why he was trying to destroy me somehow. And you can see it all through my life—how God has taken me out of danger. I also recalled the memory of when I was staying there with my cousins, so my uncle abused me, and I never told anybody. One time, he wanted me to put my hand on my aunt's private part when she was asleep. I denied doing that, and I said, "Are you crazy?"

That's how perverted he was. Though I never did that, he forced me to do it. I knew that was bad, disgusting, and awfully sick. He just wanted me to reach and touch her, but I never did.

Moreover, what I remember about my uncle was that he would sometimes take me along on his trips in the 18-wheeler, possibly for dumping sand or other materials. I was always hesitant because I feared that he might do inappropriate things with me, but my mom always pressured me to go with him. I said, "I don't want to go with him."

It was the time when that tragic accident occurred while he was dumping the dirt. Unfortunately, the electric wires were low, and when he lifted the cage to dump the dirt, he accidentally touched the live wires. The wires were not completely insulated, due to which the wires caused the glass and tires to melt and ignite, resulting in a fire. He might have been safe if he had stayed away from the area after the accident. However, he chose to return, unintentionally touching the ground and the door handle, which caused him to be electrocuted and severely burned.

When I learned about his death, the accident seemed to save me from a tragic fate. Perhaps it was a turning point where fate intervened to protect me from harm. When I received the news of his passing, I didn't feel any strong emotions, just a sense of detachment. After my uncle died, I told my mom everything. I don't think she cried or anything. My mom knew that I was gay. Later on, my mom told my aunt about the sex incident. It's unfortunate that even in death, there were legal matters to contend with, and it sounds like his family received compensation through legal proceedings. They used this money to purchase land, trailer homes, and even a house for one of his sons. I didn't choose or decide to be gay, but I accepted it regardless. I believe that God has given me a set of cards, and it's up to me to play them to the best of my ability. Another thing to consider is that I went to church and wanted guidance from God. I questioned why certain scriptures seemed to condemn individuals like me, who are gay, to hell. I even discussed this with my pastor, expressing my concerns and anxieties. However, there's a scripture that I hold dear. It says, "I will have mercy on whoever I want to have mercy, and I will forgive whomever I want to forgive because I am God, so that no one may boast and say, 'I did this and this and this.'" This scripture reminds me of God's unlimited mercy and forgiveness, giving me hope and comfort.

That scripture holds deep meaning for me. It provides comfort and assurance in my faith. I believe that God reveals the true significance of the scriptures to me through His Spirit, guiding me in understanding their relevance to my life. This personal revelation brings me peace and allows me to trust in God's mercy and forgiveness. Furthermore, I find comfort in the fact that I'm not harming anyone. I'm committed to my marriage and living a moral life according to my understanding of the Bible. I struggle to learn and grow every day, seeking wisdom from God's Word and applying it to my life. Through this continuous journey of faith, I find fulfillment and contentment. Every day, I ask

God for forgiveness for any sins I've committed against Him and His angels. This prayer brings me peace and reassurance that everything will be okay. However, for those who are experiencing abuse or uncomfortable situations, it's crucial to seek help. While faith and prayer can provide comfort, taking real-world steps to address the situation is essential. In situations like these, the only true way to find determination is by seeking answers from the Lord. God understands and knows exactly what I am going through when I am at my lowest point. I won't find comfort in idols or statues—they can't hear, see, or comfort me as Jesus can. Jesus is universal and can reach me wherever I am. People who have faced similar struggles often turn to Jesus for guidance and comfort because he's real and can provide genuine answers.

In moments of danger or hardship, it's often the presence and intervention of God that pull us through. Despite the challenges we face, God's grace and protection can be felt in tangible ways. For example, when I was on the verge of falling into the well, it was as if an unseen force prohibited me from harm, guiding me away from danger at the last moment. These experiences are powerful reminders of God's watchful care and guiding hand in our lives, providing comfort and reassurance even in the darkest times. For those who are struggling, I encourage them to seek support and guidance from trusted individuals, such as friends, family, or professionals. It's important to reach out to organizations or resources that specialize in providing assistance to those experiencing abuse or hardship. Additionally, reading the

Bible and seeking guidance from God can provide strength and clarity during difficult times. Regardless of gender, everyone is capable of sinning, as we all bleed red and are equally human. In the context of intimate relationships, both men and women may engage in sexual activities within the bounds of marriage, which God considers acceptable.

It's important not to judge or condemn others based on their actions, as everyone's journey and experiences are unique. In relationships, both partners may engage in various intimate acts, including oral sex, as part of their expression of love and intimacy. It's not productive to compare or scrutinize the actions of one gender over another, as both men and women are capable of similar behaviors. Instead, focus on fostering mutual respect, understanding, and communication within relationships, regardless of gender roles or expectations.

For younger individuals facing abuse, it's essential to speak up and seek assistance from a trusted adult, such as a parent or guardian. Don't hesitate to reach out to authorities or support services if needed. Abuse is both a sin and a crime, and perpetrators must be held accountable for their actions to prevent further harm. In today's society, there are various avenues for seeking help, including contacting the police or organizations dedicated to assisting victims of abuse. Remember, you deserve to live in safety and peace, and people and resources are available to support you through difficult times.

Chapter 4: Drugs

Like every other guy, I also expected my twenties to be the best time of my life. I should have been free, exploring and enjoying the world, and figuring out who I wanted to be. Instead of that, I felt bored and stuck. My cousin, who was always the one up for a good time, once offered me a way out. He pulled out a small bag filled with green leaves—weed, as he called it.

I didn't know much about it, but everyone seemed to be doing it. Since I didn't want to be the only one left out—the only one who said 'no'—so I took a hit. Initially, I felt it was weird and nasty. The smoke burned my throat and left, making me cough. I didn't feel much different except a little lightheaded. But it was a crack in the door, a small step down a path that would lead me far from where I wanted to be.

If you want to know the very first drug that I had, then you won't believe it. It was this stuff called linoleum, or spray paint. You huff it out of a bag with toilet paper stuffed inside. I know it sounds crazy, but guess what the worst part was? The name. It wasn't like "happy bubbles" or "cloud nine." It was just "pain." Like physical pain or maybe heartache. It made sense, though, considering the hallucinations I'd get.

So, one time, I was under a train bridge while huffing away, and I swear I saw a giant snake tongue lick my forehead. Another time, there was a UFO hovering right above me. It seemed real at the time, but it turned out that it wasn't the drugs messing with my head but a tumor right between my eyes and nose. So, I believe that the throbbing pain that shot straight to my head like a bolt of lightning was a turning point. It matched the detection of a protruding tumor. It was a growth that confirmed my deepest fear. While others offered changed descriptions, my own belief was that this was a physical manifestation of a past meeting. It was a mark left by the enemy on my body.

Soon, the school became a drag for me. My backpack felt heavy, and I couldn't seem to get enough sleep. I faced difficulty waking up for class, and it was a nightmare for me. This habit left me feeling guilty for skipping, but the thought of sitting in that stuffy classroom made me groan. It all came crashing down when the absentee officer called my mom. The judge in court yelled at me, as his words were sharp and cold. I felt ashamed of myself. This shame burned my cheeks as I realized how much trouble I was in.

As a punishment, they sent me to the Job Corps, a place where you could learn a trade. It was pretty strict, with many rules and schedules, but at least I didn't have to go to regular school anymore. That's when I saw my old friends again. They seemed different. I realized that their laughter was edgy and nervous. They were into something new—cocaine, they called it.

Cocaine scared me at first. But my friends made it sound amazing, as they told me that it gave a better high than weed. I watched them sniff the white powder with their eyes wide and crazy. It wasn't long before I was doing it, too. It wasn't like weed. It wasn't a slow, relaxed feeling. It was a jolt and a sharp hit that made me feel like I could do anything. Then came crack—the word itself sent shivers down my spine as it sounded even more dangerous than cocaine. But my friends swore it was the best. They'd take a tiny rock, heat it up in a glass pipe, and inhale the smoke. It made them act wild, jittery, and out of control, but they kept doing it. I was also attracted to it, and a part of me wanted to try it. Deep down, I knew it was wrong, as this wasn't the life I wanted. Never in my wildest dreams, I wanted to be a drug addict and hang out with people who were falling apart. But the drugs had a hold on me, as every hit was a promise of escape. It was a way to forget all my problems. Unfortunately, with each hit, I sank much deeper into a dark hole, and the hope of ever getting out seemed to fade away.

To have fun and spend some time relaxing, I started taking weed. For me, it was a harmless way to enjoy and calm my inner self with my friends. The first time I tried it, I was nervous. The smoke was so harsh, but then I started smiling and laughing at everything, even things that weren't funny. It felt good and carefree. But then that feeling didn't last. When the high wore off, I just felt tired and hungry— everyone called it the munchies. I'd eat anything I could find, like my stomach was a bottomless pit.

I remember visibly that when I was back in seventh grade, certain things at home were quite rough and rugged. My mom was constantly stressed and worried about paying the rent and bills. At the same time, my younger brothers wouldn't help out around the house. Additionally, whenever I tried to talk to her about it, she'd yell at me, and that made me feel invisible, like nobody cared about what I was going through. All this anger and sadness would build up inside me like a volcano, and I just wanted to escape far from that place. In that need and search for escape, that's when I started hanging out on the streets—smoking weed. It took the edge off and made me forget about all the problems at home for a little while. But the high never lasted long, and then I'd feel even worse than before. I knew it was wrong, but I couldn't quit it. It became a vivacious cycle: smoke weed, feel suitable for a little while, then feel even worse, then smoke more weed to escape again.

The more I smoked, the more I craved that feeling of escape. Soon, I realized that weed wasn't enough anymore. On the streets, I saw other guys smoking something different, something they called crack. They said it was a much stronger high, a way to forget everything. I was shit terrified to try it at first, but the pain and loneliness were more substantial than my fear—hence I gave it a try.

That's when things got terrible. Crack wasn't like weed. It didn't make me laugh. It just made me feel jittery and paranoid. Everywhere I looked, I saw danger, and I always felt frightened. The escape I craved turned into a prison of fear. I was utterly alone and addicted to a drug that was destroying me. One night, when I was around 24 years old, I was high as a kite and slumped in the car parked in front of my house. My house had a porch and then a narrow passage that led back to some fancy apartments. It wasn't quite an alley, but a little hidden path. Suddenly, a guy walked through that passage and headed toward the back of the apartments. I recognized him—a friend of the people who lived in one of those fancy places. Then, a crack like a firecracker split the night. The same guy stumbled back out with his face pale and tired. There was a single teardrop that was clear as day and glistened beneath his eye. Soon, the fear and the haze of drugs clouded my mind. I realized he'd been shot. Suddenly, panic surged through me, but it was mixed with a warped sense of wanting to help. After that, there was a rush of cars and cops that flooded the street with sirens wailing. Through the haze, I announced, "I know who did it! I know who did it!" This guy wasn't a nasty dude. He never caused trouble and never ripped anyone off. But I became sad seeing him like that and shot down. This triggered something in me.

They bundled me into a cop car while I was still high and shaky. At the station, there was a detective with a puffed-up chest who started questioning me. "You know who did it? You know who did it?" he kept repeating. "I'm telling you, I know who did it!" I stumbled back. He just ridiculed me, telling me to shut my mouth.

Finally, they showed me mugshots and pointed at the face that haunted my memory. I grumbled out, "That's him. That's the one who shot him." It took some time, but they eventually found the guy. He'd fled across the border and hid out near the Rio Grande in McAllen. The Rangers finally tracked him down. That night, I was high out of my mind. I witnessed a senseless tragedy. The guilt and fear of that night would stay with me for a long time. It was a plain reminder of the darkness that drugs had brought into my life.

The drugs! Of course, they changed everything in my life and my relationships with everyone. That's the reason I ended up in Oslo, far away from home. My mom never seemed to be on my side. I just wanted my brothers to help out around the house and do their part so we could escape the mess we were in. But she wouldn't listen; she wouldn't even make them try. Maybe it was because I was gay. Perhaps she had a problem with that, deep down. I don't know for sure, but it felt like she held something against me for it. And that, on top of everything else, just pushed me deeper into drugs, as it was a way to escape and numb the pain of feeling invisible and unwanted.

Despite our disagreements, the siblings ultimately put aside their differences and came together to support their family in need, proving that blood is indeed thicker than water.

So, you see, I was never the one to seek attention. I was happy to blend in and loved to be the quiet observer in the back of the room. But with my mom constantly shutting me out, I felt even more alone and depressed. Due to this, drugs became my companions in a twisted form of comfort that filled the void she left behind. Eventually, the truth about my addiction leaked out. It wasn't me who confessed, not at first. People talk, you know? Especially when they're around someone using it like I was. The news hit my family hard and shattered whatever fragile connections we had left. The impact of addiction on my family relationships, particularly with my mother, got worse. It was the feeling of being unheard and unsupported, which I attribute partly to her disapproval of my sexuality.

My journey through addiction was a dim, depressed, and lonely one, but it ultimately led me to a place of consideration and hope. So, if you're surrounded by depression and sadness, the most important thing is not to keep it bottled up inside. Know that holding onto guilt and shame will only make things worse and inferior. Therefore, finding someone you trust and believe has your best interests at heart is better. It could be anyone: your friend, a family member, a counselor, or a religious leader—whoever feels safe and supportive. It is crucial and essential for the well-being of your physical and mental health to talk things out, and sharing your struggles can be a decisive first step.

It is necessary to look for something bigger than yourself. A higher power or spiritual connection can also be a source of strength. You can also turn to prayer or meditation or explore different faiths—these are all options to consider if they resonate with you. Finally, the route to recovery is different for everyone. But don't forget that there is help accessible to everyone, and you don't have to go through this all alone. For those of you who know someone struggling with drugs, don't be scared or anxious to reach out. Let them know that you care and that you believe in them. Sometimes, a simple reminder that they are loved can be the stimulus that kindles the fight for recovery and encourages them to seek help and find a support system. Most importantly, it is crucial to believe in their capability to overcome this trial.

Always remember that there is light at the end of the tunnel, and with precise, correct help and support, anyone can break free from the grip of addiction.

Chapter 5: Prison

The winter wind whipped around me with a harsh distinction from the warmth I'd just left behind inside my house. It was a restless night with the kind that worried at your insides and wouldn't let you settle. So, I stepped outside, hoping the cool air would clear my head. It was a foolish decision, and one I'd come to regret deeply.

Just as I stood there, a figure materialized out of the shadows. A man with his face obscured by the dim streetlight. He approached me with a hurried step. His voice was a low rasp that sent shivers down my spine. "Can you hold something for me, man? Just for a minute?"

The words hung heavy in the air. Drugs. It wasn't a question, but it was more of a desperate plea that was covered in a request. My gut clenched, and a knot of unease formed in my stomach. Before I could form a proper response, I reluctantly agreed to his plea.

He explained with his voice laced with urgency that he needed a place to stash some "stuff" before a quick errand. Crack. There was no mistaking it now. The sparkle in his eyes and the desperation in his posture were enough to understand everything. It all painted a picture I desperately wished I hadn't seen. Panic bothered me at the edges of my mind, but there was a misplaced sense of obligation. I didn't want to seem like a coward, which kept me rooted to the spot. He described a rundown house on the other side of the street, which was a notorious drug den in the neighborhood.

As I crossed the street, the air swung thick with a sour stink and a mix of decay and desperation. I went inside, where the fluorescent lights buzzed overhead, casting the room in a sickly pale glow. There was desperation and nervousness on the faces, which made me more anxious. I handed over the twenty dollars he thrust into my sweaty palm, the money feeling dirty and wrong in my hand. The dealer was a broad-shouldered man with a shaved head and a scar that looked like a lightning bolt across his cheek. He tossed me a crack rock. My fingers brushed against the cold plastic, which sent a wave of nausea through me.

I hurriedly stuffed a smashed crack rock in my sock, and I clutched the other in my sweaty palm. While stepping back outside, I felt a sense of relief that momentarily erased the knot of dread in my gut. But unknowingly, that feeling was short-lived. Sirens wailed in the distance, and they grew louder with each passing second. Panic clawed at my throat as a police car shrieked to a halt in front of the drug den.

Two figures emerged, their stern faces lit by the blinking lights. "Freeze!" one of them barked with his voice, leaving no room for argument. I couldn't move, as I was scared to the core. My heart hammered against my ribs, and a panicky drum solo threatened to burst through my chest.

I managed to appear calm while my mind raced. It was a desperate scramble for escape. In a moment of pure stupidity, I threw the crack rock, and it somehow landed in the street. I swear, this cop rolled up and somehow later claimed that he found a rock right on the street where I was standing—planted evidence. These cops were dirty. If they hadn't planted it, then they couldn't have pinned anything on me, and I could have sued them. But nope, they had to cook something up. They said they found it on the pavement outside in this alley, but I know for a fact I didn't toss it. They were crooked.

"Get down on the ground! It was all that I heard in that panicky situation. The other officer shouted with a voice laced with suspicion. My hands shook as I sank to the pavement—the cold seeped into my bones. They searched me thoroughly with their rough hands, handling my pockets and purse. They found nothing. But then, unfortunately, the officer's eyes fell on the discarded bag lying forgotten on the sidewalk. A triumphant grin played on his lips as soon as he saw that bag.

He sneered while holding up the convicting evidence. I tried my best not to get caught, but it didn't work there, and that's when my world crumbled. All my naive attempts at hiding the evidence had been in vain. They hadn't found it in me, but somehow they knew.

Being already terrified, I did what I thought was needed. I denied it after being caught, but it was futile. December 1999—the day my life took a sharp turn. That day, the word echoed in my head like a death knell—possession. And just like that, I was booked into the county jail with the heavy metal doors slamming shut behind me. Following that day, freedom felt like a distant memory. The County jail wasn't exactly a vacation spot where they hooked me up with a public defender—a lawyer for people who can't afford one. The lawyer who was appointed for me shows up with a deal. It was a year in state jail or nine months in this "safety" program. "Safety" sounded unclear from the start, but nine months beats a year. Hence, I made a decision and took the deal, but then I had to wait for six long months for a spot to open up in this safety program. By the time I finally got in, I was already frustrated as hell from being stuck in a tiny cell with nothing but my thoughts. Jail was a nightmare, and that's not where I really learned about my anger issues. It was overcrowded, loud, and filled with people who'd made some grave mistakes. But for me, it became a turning point. Maybe it was hitting rock bottom, or maybe it was just having some time to think—I found myself drawn to the Bible.

Now, I wasn't some worshipper before this. I never hurt anyone. All I was trying to escape was the pain and dead-end life I was trapped in. But the Bible offered a kind of hope I hadn't found anywhere else. My pastor's words echoed in my head. He guided me to pray for understanding and wisdom that weren't in this world. Moreover, this safety program was supposed to be a breeze, but it turned out to be just another form of abuse. They had these classes where your fellow inmates would call you out on the smallest things, like when you forgot to say "excuse me" or trading candy with another dude. They even had this thing called the "cannonball," which I guess was supposed to be a sort of punishment for acting like a hotshot. I am still not sure exactly what they did in those self-defense classes, but I can't exactly talk about it. Let's just keep it this way: it wasn't pleasant. After all that, they shipped me off to a special program in Lubbock for people with mental health problems. It turns out that all the jail time messed me up, and I got diagnosed with depression, bipolar disorder, and the whole shebang. This new place was like a handicapped facility, but with classes. I ended up losing it there, too, after which they transferred me to another place closer to home for people with mental illness who take medication. This place wasn't exactly luxurious at all. Imagine waking up at 5 a.m. to the smell of cow poop, but at least it wasn't a cell. It was more like a dorm room, which was a step up. I lasted there for almost a year before I finally got out, but even then, I had to go through a halfway house program.

I stayed for six months in near-isolation, with only one hour a day outside my cell. It wasn't ideal, obviously, but it gave me time to reflect on my life and the path I wanted to take. It was a long road ahead, but at least I knew where I was headed—to a rehab center as a chance to finally break free from the cycle of addiction and violence. The wait for a bed in the rehab program felt like an eternity. Six months in solitary confinement may have been rough, but at least I knew what I was facing. Here, it was a waiting game.

Those six months in solitude weren't easy. It was a tiny cell with a shower and a toilet, and I spent 23 hours a day locked inside. The only human interaction I had was with a guy named Selly on the other side of the wall. We'd talk through the vents, sharing stories, and he would give me books to read that helped me pass the time. There were different types of people in that jail. Some were in for petty theft, while others were in for something much worse. One guy, I remember, looked weighed down by a sadness so deep it seemed to crush him. I inquired about him, and it turned out that he was in for murder.

Despite the circumstances, I also saw a glimmer of hope for him. I asked him if he'd be interested in reading the Bible together, as I was hoping to offer some comfort. I wanted to tell him that God loves you and that even your murder can be forgiven. I wasn't sure if he'd believe me, but something deep inside me urged me to try. He agreed to that, and during those breaks, when we were allowed out of our cells, we'd study the scriptures. It was so good to dedicate our time to reading the Bible. We'd gather in his cell; he even offered me a seat. I almost felt like I was teaching him. I was sitting across from this guy. I felt like I should be the one explaining things and teaching him something. He wasn't there for a heart-to-heart. I was the only one offering comfort, which felt crazy considering he was charged with murder.

I felt the Holy Spirit with me. It was a comforting presence that raced away the fear, even though I was sitting across from someone who was charged with murder. It turned out he was a witness to the murder he was charged with. Someone else had committed the crime, but he knew too much, and they wanted him silenced. He told me everything with a raw fear in his voice. One day, everything went sideways. This guy, the one I was trying to help, suddenly pulled out a temporary weapon—a shank from a razor and a toothbrush. He admitted that someone had put a hit on me, and he was supposed to be the one to do it. He called for the guards to open the cell, and here's the thing: it felt way too easy. Maybe the guard was on it. Why else would he open the cell so readily when all the others were locked tight?

Somehow, I got out of that situation alive and safe. Maybe it was divine involvement, or maybe it was just dumb luck. But at that moment, I really felt a rush of gratitude for whatever hidden force had protected me. They put me in protective custody, and I knew the Lord had delivered me from that. That close call landed me in protective custody, for which I am grateful. The whole incident landed him in jail, where he ended up serving seven or eight years. He told me this not as a complaint but as a cautionary tale. It was a stark reminder of how quickly things could go south, even with good intentions.

My time in solitary wasn't wasted either. The experience definitely changed me. It was in that tiny cell, with only my thoughts and the occasional conversation with Selly, that I learned to identify my triggers. Anger, arguments, having money in my pocket, and all those things could send me spiraling back to drugs. It was a valuable lesson and one that I will never forget. When I finally got transferred to the rehab program, I carried that knowledge with me, and a new chapter was started. I took it as a chance to finally break free from the cycle of addiction.

Chapter 6: Safeway House

The role of the church greatly impacted my upbringing. When it came to my sexuality, I had concerns about how people at the church would think about my homosexuality. I was struggling with the idea of confessing it in church; therefore, I approached the pastor for guidance. I find his response not only comforting but also thoughtful and understanding. The pastor emphasized God's forgiveness and mercy and advised me to be cautious about sharing this personal aspect of my life with others in the church. His words helped me find peace, after which I decided to leave this matter to God.

In my daily routine, I always try to be a better person. I struggle to represent kindness and compassion and believe in helping others without seeking recognition or praise. When I have the means, I make it a point to support those in need within my community and beyond. It always feels good to help others.

So, when I went to jail for drug-related reasons, I suffered several disturbing experiences related to my pituitary tumor, including two instances where I lost consciousness and required emergency medical attention. The first one occurred while I was imprisoned, when my head hurt so bad that I passed out in the infirmary. They assumed that I had gone, so the guards rushed me to the hospital, where I received C.P.R. and recovered consciousness. Another incident happened when I was en route to the hospital—the ambulance had to stop at a gas station due to a faulty light. Each time my tumor acted up, it caused unbearable pain for me. During one ambulance ride, a female paramedic mocked my pain, which was so inconsiderate. Whereas the lead paramedic numbed me, which led me to dream and become disoriented. I was hearing as well as I could see the operating light despite being sedated. More or less, it was like an alien ship, and everyone there was so rude. Despite the trauma and suffering, I chose not to sue them.

However, I shared my experiences with my lawyer, which likely influenced the court's decision to grant me time served. Through these trials, I've come to realize that a higher power has consistently interfered on my behalf and guided me through the darkest moments. Things changed quite easily when I came back.

Although I was already attending church, there was a particular incident when I felt the Holy Spirit, and that turned my life around. I was still struggling with addiction, but the experience led me to leave it behind. I already admit that I'm not perfect, and thankfully, I've been saved numerous times by the Lord. I still continue to struggle, but I find comfort in knowing that God is always with me and forgives me.

Here, the important thing to remember is that none of us are perfect and holy. Everyone is going through their own struggles and sins, and it's just that we are forgiven. Therefore, accepting the Lord as your Savior and developing a deep personal relationship with God is what truly matters more than just following a religion. His sacrifice on the cross was meaningful, and if you accept Him with your heart and confess with your mouth that He is your Lord and Savior, you will be forgiven. I admit that I have often turned my back on him and felt bad. But the Lord was so kind that He never abandoned me. I want to make it clear that I am not without fault; I am a sinner, just like anyone else. However, I am grateful for having someone to turn to for forgiveness, as promised in the Bible. Amidst everything, the most powerful experience that I've had was feeling the presence of the Lord in that room, which brought me closer to God than ever before. It was a clear indication that the Lord was with me at that moment. My relationship with God is strong enough that I feel His presence in my life. I believe that every success, twist of fate, and lesson in my life that I have learned all point to His glory. Since the glory of God is a powerful way to express your faith and gratitude, I attribute all the glory to God. He orchestrated the meeting between Johnny and me and helped me overcome my addiction.

Otherwise, it would have been impossible. Johnny was there, but God placed him there, and he is just a vessel like me. Who overcame my addiction? Jesus. Furthermore, he promises to never forsake me. If anyone turns their back on me, we leave them behind. I was. I wonder. Well, I said, but one. At one point last year, I expressed my frustration. Then I made a decision. I asked the Lord for help because I couldn't do it on my own. And now it has come to pass. I've been clean. I got his blessings. Life is full of wonderful and wonder-filled moments, and it is important to remember each one! It is also filled with many challenging times when we must hold on to our faith, His grace, and all that is good in our lives just to take our next breath. His grace is sufficient for every situation, to the glory of God, whose grace carried me through darkness and into the light. So when I returned from jail, I was searching for a yard to work on and earn some money. So, I visited Johnny's house. At first, his brother declined, but then Johnny himself came out eventually, and we had a good conversation. Since we lived close by, I used to visit a music store called Rosenberg Music Company. There, I met Miss Sims, who was the owner's mother. She allowed me to run the store and sell guitars and guitar strings. So that's how I got the job. As I worked there, I also learned to play the piano with lessons from Miss Turner. I started learning contemporary Christian music.

Afterward, I gradually learned to play different genres that also included lullabies. So, during my off time at work, I taught myself how to play and practiced in the piano room when it was empty. Eventually, I found out that Johnny had also visited the store, and then again, we had a conversation. Later, he entrusted me with his phone while he was at work, and our relationship grew from there.

We also bought a car that was solely for transportation from point A to point B. My concerns were about becoming a father and fulfilling that role. Unfortunately, my brother was involved in a situation where his girlfriend, with whom he had three kids, separated due to domestic issues. That's how I ended up taking care of the youngest child,

Christopher who was about a year old. So we used to take him with us everywhere we went. We took him with us when we used to deliver newspapers for Ben Harold. I always prayed to have a child, which was somehow fulfilled when I got to take care of my brother's son. I was more than happy to fulfill the role of father. It was a realization that my prayers had been answered in the form of Christopher.

So, time passed, and we took care of him until he was about five years old. Christopher was a grown-up kid now. We made sure to provide infinite love and support for him. However, sadly, his mother eventually decided to take him back. That was the worst thing that shattered me. Although we didn't ask for anything in return, we still extended our help when needed because we felt it was good to be helpful.

At one point in my life, I felt inspired to take food to underprivileged children in Mexico since I had gone through that phase. Therefore, I made several trips to Mexico with clothes and food. The immigration authorities took my green card away. It was a shocking disappointment that left me feeling lost and perplexed. It happened over 20 years ago after they discovered a felony principle on my record, thus making me unqualified for permanent residency. They told me to appear before an immigration judge, but I never received any official notification or any such paperwork. Despite the delay, I tried my best to move forward and do everything in my power to maintain my identity and status. It was a difficult and frustrating time, but I endured. And then, just last month, after two decades of ambiguity, I finally received my green card back. It was a moment of huge relief and gratitude. I would say that it was the proof of my determination, as I was trying my best to do what I could to identify myself through those years.

Additionally, I felt a strong connection to the teachings of the Bible. I find this scripture really close to my heart:

Roman 9:15

"For he says to Moses, "I will have mercy on whom I have mercy, and I will have compassion on whom I have compassion." (NIV)

This verse from Romans 1:15 (NIV) touches on the concept of God's sovereignty in showing mercy. Here, God tells Moses that He will choose to be merciful and compassionate towards whomever He decides. This doesn't mean God is arbitrary or unfair. The passage is more about emphasizing God's ultimate authority and highlighting that salvation is a gift from Him, not something we can earn. It doesn't necessarily address specific human actions or behaviors.

Chapter 7: Love

As I think about love, I realize that it's not something that you force someone to get. It happens naturally. It's not about having someone present by your side, but it's more than that. Basically, it's about having someone who genuinely cares for you and looks out for your well-being. It's about someone who sticks by your side through thick and thin and, no matter what, never leaves you alone.

Someone wouldn't even, in the wildest dream, think of harming you or being the reason for your sadness. For me, love is pure, genuine care without any motives. Just a raw, love-filled feeling for a person, like a donut being filled with the yummiest Boston cream. That's what love means to me—two beautiful people taking care of each other and supporting each other throughout. Moreover, I've learned this from my family, especially my grandparents, who taught me the importance of sacrifice and putting others first.

The presence of my husband, Johnny, in my life is no less than a blessing. We met at church. I am thankful to God that we met because, since we met, he's always helped me through tough times. My family accepted me and John. They have no issues with my sexuality.

They like Johnny, and I think that's great because he took me out of that mess. He helped me out a lot. They didn't approve of our relationship, and we've faced their criticism together. John's been my rock since the beginning, and I'm grateful for his support. I have a deep sense of responsibility and love for my family, and I've always been there for them, even when things get tough. I've helped them out in countless ways, and to this day, I continue to care for them. I still made sure that they were okay, even when I was building a life with John. My mom holds a special place in my heart, and despite everything I've been through, she's still my priority. I always make sure to put her needs first.

My grandparents and the Bible have taught me the importance of family and taking care of one another. I strive to live by those values. But his family is not like that, and they don't like him being with me—none of them. They all have two faces, and they have tried really hard to tear us apart. They always complain about why he is not taking care of his mother, and they don't care about her. So that's how they try to get in between us.

Conversely, my family never showed any rudeness toward our relationship because he had always helped me overcome my shortcomings, including my struggles with addiction. I'm proud to say that I've been drug-free for a year now. For me, it's a remarkable achievement that I will cherish forever. I overcame my addiction and the challenges that I faced after my accident, which left me reliant on opioids like fentanyl patches.

But in spite of the struggles, I've remained committed to my recovery and refused to let drugs control my life again. It's evidence of the power of faith and the support of loved ones like John, who helped me through the darkest times. Since childhood, my grandfather and grandmother have instilled in me a strong sense of compassion, empathy, and responsibility, and I'm grateful for their guidance and love. Furthermore, the Bible has also been a source of comfort and wisdom, and it reminds me to honor my parents and care for my family. So, even when it gets challenging, I know that I'm doing the right thing by putting my family first and the rest of them second. I also had a dear friend named Brian, who was also gay and played the piano at a Presbyterian Church. We met through mutual friends and shared our experiences. We spent time together, discovering Houston and even visiting a gay club on South Beach.

Brian was such a kind soul, and we thoroughly enjoyed each other's company. Unfortunately, he passed away due to COVID-19. I cherished the memories we made together, including our bingo nights, which often ended in us winning and stirring up controversy. We didn't let the criticism get us down, though. I'm a stubborn person who refuses to be told what to do or how to act. Johnny, on the other hand, is more reserved and prefers to avoid conflict. In spite of our differences, we've found a loving and supportive partnership with each other.

On Tuesday night, I attended a prayer service and felt drawn to the prayer room. As I prayed, I was overcome with a burst of uncontrollable laughter that lasted for about half an hour. There were tears that streamed down my face as I laughed uncontrollably, and I simply couldn't explain why. The two brothers present recognized the Holy Spirit's presence and jokingly told me to "leave some for them."

They understood well that I was experiencing a moment of divine joy and completely surrendering to it. Johnny was there, too, and we shared in the joy and wonder of that moment. It was a beautiful experience that I'll never forget, and it strengthened my connection with my faith and the power of the Holy Spirit. John and I have shared many adventures throughout our journey. We went on a cruise to Cayman Island, Cozumel, Mexico, and Kingston, Jamaica. We also went to Vegas and Disney World, apart from enjoying quiet moments at home. We've had our ups and downs, but our love has endured everything that comes our way.

Chapter 8: Ambulance Incident

One day, when I was driving back from Walmart, I noticed my headlights weren't working properly. As I was heading home, I spotted a police officer in the distance. It was maybe ten blocks away. I knew that familiar sight all too well. As I turned around, he flipped on his lights and pulled me over at a nearby gas station. My heart began to race as I felt my tumor starting to act up. It triggered my anxiety and depression. I panicked while thinking, "Here we go again." The officer approached me, and he mentioned something about a ticket or fine. I was a mess as my mind raced with worst-case scenarios.

Oh God, no, please, not jail! I blurted out in panic. My license had expired, and I was terrified. My tumor was acting up, and I felt myself spiraling into a familiar void of anxiety and depression. I begged the officer to call an ambulance. I tried explaining to him that my tumor caused me to see white dots and feel faint. But he just didn't believe me, which was rude and insensitive. He thought I was trying to twist out of a ticket. I pleaded with him, "I've been to the emergency room. I have proof! Please, just listen!" But he remained skeptical until, finally, he sympathized and called for an ambulance. I was in agony as my body and mind screamed for relief.

As they loaded me into the ambulance, frustration grew within me. "Come on, why are we still here? Can't we just get to the emergency room already?" But the paramedics seemed skeptical, thinking I was faking my symptoms. One of them was a woman who even sarcastically chimed in, "Oh, I have a tumor too." I felt my anger rise. "You're being facetious! You don't understand what I'm going through." The lead paramedic interfered and sternly told me to quiet down and administer a shot that left me passing out every two minutes. It was a terrifying and humiliating experience, as I felt like no one believed me or took my condition seriously.

I didn't realize I had blacked out until I was trapped in a dream in which I was desperate to wake up. I knew something was wrong, but my body felt heavy and unresponsive. I tried to move my mouth, but it felt like slow motion. The next thing I knew, a strange and otherworldly noise surrounded me. It was like the sound effects from a sci-fi movie. Then, a bright light filled my vision, and I slowly began to come to it. As I regained consciousness, I found myself in an operating room that was surrounded by the familiar sights of medical equipment and the bright round lamps overhead. Surely, it was a confusing and frightening experience. I felt like I was trapped in a nightmare from which I couldn't escape.

I regained consciousness and opened my eyes. I felt like I was in a spaceship, with bright lights shining down on me. But the reality was far more disturbing. I was handcuffed to a hospital bed and surrounded by medical staff who seemed more interested in treating me like a criminal than a patient in need. The same unconcerned and rude behavior followed me to the county jail, as it was the place where I was met with cruelty and neglect. When I was first taken to the county jail, the guards and nurses didn't believe me when I told them about my tumor. They thought I was faking it and didn't care about my well-being. I felt like I was under so much pressure, and no one was listening. It got to the point where I felt overwhelmed and said something about hurting myself. The next thing I knew, they stripped me down and restrained me. They threw me in a cell like an animal, and it was so humiliating and painful.

I've been through a lot and tried to stay humble, but it's hard when people treat you like you're less than human. I believe that some of those guards and nurses have their own secrets and sins, and they haven't been caught yet. But God sees everything, and they will answer to Him one day. They may think they're above the law, but they're just ignorant of the truth. They don't know the power of God's judgment and mercy.

Even in the hospital, the nurses were heartless and unprofessional. I pleaded with them while explaining that I was still suffering from my tumor, but they just dismissed me. Eventually, they took me to a gurney, where my high blood pressure spiked, and the tumor's symptoms overwhelmed me once again, knocking me out. It was a never-ending cycle of trauma and neglect, with no one willing to listen or help. I passed out and was unconscious for a few minutes. I thought I had died. However, the medical staff revived me. They used compression techniques on my chest, after which they quickly realized that they couldn't keep me in the facility due to liability concerns. So, they released me the next day, and I went home. This was yet another instance where my life was in danger, and I had proof of the neglect and mistreatment that I suffered. It's not just a story; it's a documented reality. I'm not having these experiences. In fact, they're proof of my resilience and willpower to share my truth. I'm so grateful to have God by my side through all my struggles. I want to share my story to show others that trusting God is everything to me. I'm the type of person who will give someone the benefit of the doubt and turn the other cheek more than once. But when someone keeps pushing and it becomes unfair, I will stand up for myself. I won't let others keep hurting me without speaking out. I'm not a pushover and won't be taken advantage of. I trust God to guide me and give me the strength to stand up for myself when necessary.

Talking about strength, I remember a painful incident with my cousin, who was the son of the man who raped me. He was drunk and wanted to fight me. He taunted me about not taking care of my mom. He knew about the trauma I had suffered, yet he used it against me. I tried to ignore him, but he kept pushing my buttons. Finally, he wanted to fight physically, and I was tempted to release my anger. But something inside me shifted when he told me to 'break his ribs.' I realized I was functioning out of rage and didn't want to sink to his level. So, I stopped, and surprisingly, he backed off. He didn't even compliment my strength. It was a moment of clarity that showed me that I didn't have to engage in his toxic behavior. I could rise above it and choose a different path. Well, all three males got the same issue as my raper. So, one girl scratched me when I was living in the trailer. I was little, and there was so much hate. Well, they knew I was an intruder; I guess even though I was being abused, I was the bad kid. So much hate in this world it's incomprehensible. One male, I believe, is the middle child. Thought very little of me, like I was worthless. He gave me that impression. He believed that I should help my mother, which I always did. Yet there was jealousy from them. I guess because I was a very attractive male. That they wanted to ruin my life. I have been with my other half for 20-plus years. So, they knew I had a very good chance of having a family.

Even though I was very upset at first, GOD gave me that chance to know how it feels to be a dad with me and Johnny. Having that come to a reality, I feel that Dad experienced it with my brother's son—Christopher. I thank GOD. He has never abandoned me, and I hope that whoever is going through tough situations, no matter what it is. If you hold on to JESUS hand no matter who you are. He will never let go. You can let go, but he doesn't. This is me, and I will never change. I'm a very humble person. I have learned a lot through the years that GOD has lent me.

Usually, I'm the type to turn the other cheek and let God handle it. I believe in letting Him take care of justice. But there are times when people just keep pushing and pushing until I reach my breaking point. It's like a time bomb waiting to explode. And when it does, it's not a pretty good sight to experience. I think anyone can relate to that feeling when you're pushed to the limit, and something inside you just snaps.

That's what happened in this situation. Moreover, I would like to talk about my pastor. He was a nice and humble man from Mexico who truly served God. He doesn't preach about money or material wealth, like some other pastors do. Instead, he teaches us straight from the Bible while carefully explaining each scripture and connecting it to others to show us the bigger picture. He encourages us to ask God for wisdom and understanding and trusts that the Holy Spirit will guide us. I have learned so much from him, and I admire how he stays true to his values. Even when a church member made a mistake, he addressed it with kindness and integrity. He has always shown us that we all need to walk in a straight line and follow God's path. I have so much respect for my pastor and the way he serves God with humility and elegance.

The Holy Spirit convicted him of maintaining high standards, and that meant not allowing individuals to lead worship or preach if they weren't living according to God's will. My only desire was to experience the Holy Spirit's presence in a more tangible way, as I had seen in Pentecostal churches. I yearned for that deeper connection, that tangible sense of the Holy Spirit's power and guidance. I was drawn to the Pentecostal churches because of their lively expressions of worship. They would jump up and down, and they praised God with passion and energy. I could feel the Holy Spirit's presence in the room. It was like a tangible force that was sometimes stronger and sometimes gentler but always palpable. I wanted to experience that deep connection with God and feel His Spirit moving through me in a powerful way.

I've experienced the genuine presence of the Holy Spirit, and it's unforgettable. While some may go through the motions, I've felt the real deal. I have experienced the laughter, the joy, and the sense of connection with something greater. It's like conversing with God Himself, and it's awe-inspiring. In those moments, I know that God is real, and I feel seen, heard, and understood. It's a deep sense of connection that I can't find anywhere else. It's like having a direct line to the divine, and it's the most amazing feeling in the world.

My connection with God is personal, through Jesus Christ. It's not about religion; it's actually about relationships. I understand how people can get confused and think Jesus is just a prophet or a good teacher. But for me, He's the Son of God—the flesh-and-blood manifestation of God's love. That's why I wanted a community where I could experience God's presence freely and without any restrictions. I wanted to feel the liberty to praise, to worship, and to connect with others who share my passion for God.

At first, I found it challenging to find a church that allowed for that kind of freedom, but eventually, I met Johnny at a church that felt different. The older people there had an inspiring depth of understanding and a passion for prayer. And when we came together as a group, singing and worshiping, I could feel the Holy Spirit's presence in a powerful way.

That's how I feel about my walk with God, as it's a personal and imperfect journey. I've stumbled along the way. I have fallen many times and made several mistakes, but he's always helped me get back up. Sometimes, I've returned to old patterns, but God has been patient and faithful. He has always encouraged me to move forward. And I'm grateful to say that, by His grace, I've been able to break free from those harmful habits and have been living in victory for over a year now. It's a daily choice, but God's presence and strength make all the difference. Before I knew God, my half-sister and I used to visit tarot card readers who would tell us that someone had placed a curse on us. They'd say that someone had used graveyard dirt and bones to harm us, which is a common belief in Mexico. I think my half-sister may have done that out of anger when we left Mexico. She stayed behind with her family. But now, as a Christian, I know that those beliefs are not based on truth. Since I've learned to trust in God's protection and love, I've forgiven my half-sister and anyone else who may have tried to harm me. I know that God's power is greater than any curse or negative force.

Even now, I think that my half-sister may still be trying to harm me with her curses and spells, but I stand firm on God's promises. The Bible says that any weapon formed against me will not prosper, and I believe that with all my heart. I pray for God's protection and ask Him to send angels to surround me and keep me safe. I trust in His word, as I know that He is always with me and never leaves or forsakes me. I forgive my half-sister, not because she deserves it but because God's love and grace require me to. We're not fighting against people, but we are fighting against principalities and powers against the devil, who seeks to steal, kill, and destroy. But he's a defeated enemy, and we have the victory in Jesus. We may stumble and sin, but God's mercy and forgiveness are always available to us. We're not perfect, but we're forgiven, and that's all that matters.

What I've learned in church is that the Holy Spirit has revealed to me that it's not by my own strength or understanding but by His guidance that I've come to know God's truth. I've learned that if I neglect to pray daily, the Spirit withdraws, and I feel His absence. But He always comes back to remind me to communicate with God, warning me that if I don't listen, consequences may follow. And sadly, I've experienced that firsthand; I've seen it happen when I didn't pray or listen to the Holy Spirit's nudges. It's a hard lesson to learn, but one that's taught me to never take God's presence for granted. Now, I make it a priority to talk to God daily, knowing that the Holy Spirit is my guide and my comforter.

Chapter 9: The Accident

My life has been a continuous series of disastrous events. So, that wasn't the first time I faced an issue in my life. My tumor likes to act up when I am feeling down. It made me see little dots everywhere. That night, I wasn't feeling good at all. The tumor was bothering me, as it was making me uncomfortable.

Since it was super late—around 3 or 4 in the morning—I decided to step outside and check the mailbox. I was hoping some fresh air would help. Our trailer is way back at the end of the street, with mailboxes at the very back, too. Hence, I walked over to the mailboxes. But on my way back, I started seeing those dots again. By the time I got close to the house, I knew I was in trouble, as it was getting worse. I kneeled down because I felt like I was going to faint, so I sat there and then. And sure enough, I passed out right there, so that's where I was when I passed out.

Johnny must have come looking for me. The next thing I know, as far as I remember, is the underside of his SUV, the wheels, and stuff. He stopped a little ways ahead, like ten feet or so. It seemed like he knew he had hit something. Anyway, I gathered up the courage and tried to get up, thinking I was alright. But unfortunately, my left foot wouldn't hold me. I couldn't stand it at all. That's when I knew something was wrong. My leg felt numb. I remember yelling, "Call an ambulance! We need an ambulance!"

Feeling so helpless, I just laid back down on the street. I remember someone coming out of their house and asking if I was okay. I mumbled, "Yeah," because they just went back inside. Finally, I don't know who called the ambulance, but it showed up. I remember a paramedic cutting my clothes off. The adrenaline kicks in really hard when you get hurt badly in an accident or something. That's probably why I said I was okay at first. I was not in my senses.

Anyway, they were saying I was bleeding from my head, somewhere around my forehead. Surprisingly, I didn't feel the pain at that moment, but after a while, it hit me like a ton of bricks. I remember the cops trying to calm me down as they were saying everything would be alright. Then the ambulance guys came and hooked me up to all sorts of things, like I.V.s. They put me in the ambulance, but instead of going straight to the hospital, which was ten blocks away, they took me to a helicopter that was waiting.

It was crazy. They strapped me in and everything, but I wasn't scared. It's weird, but I felt peaceful. I can't remember much after that. In my half-awake sense, I only remember the feeling of them saying, "Everything's going to be okay."

During that time, I was lost and not in my senses. At that moment, I wasn't thinking about Johnny, my mom, or my family—none of them. It was just me and that weird feeling of peace. Everything felt peaceful, even in that crazy helicopter. I tried looking out the window but couldn't move much. All I saw were lights because it was still dark out.

Anyhow, they took me to the Downtown Medical Center in Houston. That's all I remember until the next day. Apparently, I was out cold the whole time. Johnny said I was in surgery for like 8 straight hours. And when I finally woke up, I found out that I had nine broken ribs. My femur, which is the big bone in your thigh, was shattered. And my pelvis was broken, too. They had to reconstruct everything with titanium. It was like some kind of robot surgery. They put this whole contraption on my foot to keep my leg straight while it healed. They did it while I was awake. And with all that damage—especially the broken ribs—it was so hard to breathe. They put balloons under my chest, on each side, to kind of hold my ribs up, but it still wasn't enough. My oxygen was low. They wanted to put a tube down my throat to help me breathe, but I wouldn't let them. I just kept saying, "No, no." It was the most painful phase of my life. I was afraid that I would never recover from it or that I could never walk again.

Hence, I started doing physical therapy exercises myself. These were some of the little things that helped me regain my strength. But my left leg, the one with the shattered femur, still felt like it had a thousand pounds on it. I couldn't even lift it an inch. So, I guess the femur wasn't fully healed yet. And I ended up staying in the hospital for a whole month.

During that time, they took things slow. One surgery at a time, as I was on a lot of pain medications—so most of the time, I just felt numb. The only real pain came when they tried to move me, like for baths and other examinations. They'd use these special boards with straps, but it was so painful that just thinking about it sent shivers down my spine.

All of this happened four years ago, in 2020, when I was around 54 years old. So, back in the hospital, whenever they tried to help me move, it wasn't less than torture for me. It hurt so bad that I'd tell them to wait. Most of the time, I would tell them to give me some pain medication at least 20 or 30 minutes before they tried anything. But they wouldn't listen. They just did whatever they wanted, and it made me so mad.

My sister even got upset with them for not relieving me properly. They kept saying things like, "We gave you some love," which didn't help. It felt more like they were trying to control me than anything. There were times when I thought I might not make it. I wasn't exactly scared of dying, but I wasn't sure what was going to happen next.

Strangely enough, despite all that pain, there was a weird sense of peace, as I wasn't afraid. It was like everything went blank. There were no worries or anything. I wasn't scared of what might happen next. It was just... peaceful. Even though I wasn't in pain, it was terrifying. I remember watching them drill holes in my foot—yikes! It left a scar, which I still have to this day.

The worst of the pain lasted for about two or three weeks. For that whole month in the hospital, I was stuck in bed when I was barely able to breathe. They had that tube down my throat for a few days at most, but then they took it out. That's when they decided to do this new surgery, where they put plates on my ribs to help me breathe better. Apparently, it worked because that's when I finally started being able to breathe easier.

So, I was only in the hospital for a month, but I still had rehab to go to after that. They did all three surgeries at different times. Even though I was struggling to breathe, they went ahead and fixed my femur first, then the ribs, and finally the pelvis. Honestly, I wasn't even scared during the surgeries. It wasn't because I didn't care, but I couldn't feel anything. Everything was numb. Even though I wasn't feeling any pain, I remember telling them things—stuff that didn't make any sense. Thinking back, I've been through a lot in my life. I have been through so many ups and downs. There is so much stress and hardship. This accident was definitely the worst physically, while other times were no less. Being in jail was also the worst phase that messed with me mentally. But this time, the physical pain was brutal.

After the hospital, I was taken to Encompass Rehab, where I had a cozy room and three meals a day. The therapists put me through my paces, starting with exercises like getting in and out of a car, then graduating to walking with a walker in circles, and eventually tackling the stairs. It wasn't easy, but the staff were all so kind and encouraging. I could even jam out to my favorite tunes while working out a little joy that kept me going! I have to admit, I forgot my trainers' names, but they were all amazing. It took me another month to get back on my feet, but I did it! And let me tell you, it was a struggle to get the doctors to sort out my medication, but I persevered. I'm so grateful to God for seeing me through that terrible accident. Everyone was amazed that I got a second chance at life, and I knew I was meant to make the most of it. I've been through so much, but my faith has kept me strong. I give God glory every day for His blessings and mercy.

This little fake car had doors, and you would practice getting in and out. It helped. Then I did the stairs. There were three going up and three going down, and I would walk those too. Sure enough, after three weeks, I was done. I was done! I hadn't been home for two whole months, away from John. That's right, two months. So yeah, I wanted to go home. Everyone was surprised by my recovery. "Michael," they said, "God gave you another chance!" "Oh, I know he did," I replied. "Why? Maybe because of what I'm doing right now—writing a book about my life and giving Him the glory.

And maybe some kids out there—whoever's going through a tough situation—you know, there's a lot of addiction problems going on. Well, hopefully this will help them get off that stuff and try something else. I mean, I tried Jesus, and it works. You know, God knows what will come out of my book, but I'm thinking something good. If it helps just one person with their addiction, that's more than enough for me. So, finally, I recovered and started walking again. Everyone says that it was a miracle, but I don't believe in miracles. More than miracles, I believe in God's plan for everything we do. I believe God has a plan for everyone, be it your enemy, friend, or whoever that is. They might try to hurt you, but God, no, that's not his style.

That's why I believe I'm still here. I've got a lot of living left to do. Honestly, I don't dwell on the bad stuff. I believe that the negative things in your life are not worth discussing. Instead, I try to focus on what's good and positive and, above all, what God wants me to do.

I do believe that suffering isn't a respecter of faith. Even pastors who dedicate their lives to a higher power still face hardship. This puts my own troubles in perspective. I understand that life's a messy business, and complaining won't change the tide. So, maybe it's time to adopt a new tactic to face challenges head-on and see what strength I can find within myself. I'm grateful to be out of rehab and walking again, thanks to the Lord. However, I'm still dealing with chronic pain from scars on my back, femur, shoulder, and ribs. I need to find a pain management doctor to oversee my treatment. Unfortunately, I've had a tough time finding a doctor who will prescribe the medication I need. One doctor told me I didn't need the medication, saying it was only for cancer patients. Another doctor finally prescribed Fentanyl patches but then dismissed me because he was retiring. I was in a tough spot until I found Dr. Karim Azim at Greater Texan Health. He's been a wonderful doctor, understanding my situation in every way. He reviewed my surgery report and replaced my medication. Now, he's picking up where the previous doctor left off. However, I recently encountered another hurdle when my pharmacy, H.E.B., didn't have my Fentanyl patches in stock. The pharmacist seemed more concerned about their license than my well-being. It's frustrating to be judged and assumed to be looking for narcotics every time I'm in pain.

I've been through a lot, including jail time, and have learned from my mistakes. I've written a book to share my experiences and warn others to stay out of jail. My message is simple: stay out of jail and don't make the same mistakes that I did.

I'm so grateful to God for carrying me through every up and down in my life and leading me to this moment. I know that without Him, I'm nothing. He's the one who's given me strength, hope, and a second chance. I'm humbled and thankful for His love and guidance, and I acknowledge that every breath I take is a gift from Him. He's been my rock, my savior, and my everything. I'm just a vessel for His grace and mercy, and I praise Him for all He's done in my life.

Chapter 10: The Tumor

In the year 2000, I had a hospital visit that led to a surprising discovery. A C.A.T. scan revealed a pituitary tumor, but thankfully, it was benign. It was about the size of a quarter, and I suspect the intense pain might have caused it. I was experiencing at the time—flashback to the mid-1980s, around 1985, when I was living in Eagle Lake. I got caught up in a situation that was extensive in town at the time, and everyone was doing it. It was like a war, and I was swept up in the chaos. There was no off-season and no break from the action. It was an unrestrained period in my life, but I made it through.

It was a specific era!

It was a time when people were using Rust-Oleum, which was a particular brand of paint that was popular for altered states. It was the go-to paint for that purpose, and unlike other brands, that wouldn't work. And that's when I started seeing strange things, such as flying saucers and strange creatures under the bridge. It was a wild time in my life. But one experience stands out. I saw a demon-like figure—a snake licking my forehead—right in front of me. It was terrifying. And now, I realize that this was likely a manifestation of the pituitary tumor that was growing inside me, affecting my perceptions and experiences.

It turned out that the nickel-sized pituitary tumor was the root cause of my struggles. Ever since then, I've been dealing with devastating headaches and pain that would leave me passing out. I remember one particular accident or wreck. I recalled going outside at night and experiencing these strange episodes where I'd see tiny black-and-white dots. It was like spots or flashes of light. These visions would overwhelm me, and I'd end up passing out in bed. It was the most terrifying and disorienting experience. The sensations would move up and down my body like a wave of pain and discomfort. I recognized the signs, and I knew what was happening. It felt like someone was hitting me with a heavy object like a bed or a rock, and it was accompanied by sharp, stabbing sensations. When the pain became too much, I would pass out. But before losing consciousness, I would see visions of dogs. That's how intense and real the experiences were. It was like I was living in a nightmare, and I couldn't escape.

It wasn't just the physical pain, as I was also struggling with depression and bipolar disorder. These conditions would worsen the symptoms, hence making it feel like everything was hitting at once. The diagnosis happened at Oak Bend Hospital in Rosenberg, where I was living at the time. Interestingly, my struggles with depression started when I was in jail, and that's when the tumor began to grow. I remember the day I got arrested and booked. I was in so much pain from the tumor that I told the authorities about it. And then, suddenly, the pain stopped.

Then they transferred me to the medical unit. I was taken there, waiting for Johnny to bail me out. But before that could happen, the symptoms started again. It wasn't long ago that my children had been bothering me, and I was overwhelmed with emotion, crying, and everything. By the time they took me out of my cell to see the nurse, I was a mess. They placed me on one of those hospital beds. Just like they have in jail medical units with plastic mattresses and handcuff restraints. And then, suddenly, I passed out. I didn't have a pulse, so they started performing emergency procedures on me. They did chest compressions and used a defibrillator. It was one of those machines that shocked your heart to get it beating again. They worked on me for a while, and eventually, I woke up.

So that's when I technically died for a short period of time. I'm not sure how long, but it felt like infinity. It was a harrowing experience, but surprisingly, I didn't have any further complications after that incident. They released me from jail and sent me to the hospital, where I was treated and eventually sent home. I suppose the authorities wanted to avoid any potential liability if I had died in their custody. But all of this—the hospital visit, the diagnosis, and the cardiac arrest—it's all documented in my medical records and other official papers, so there's no way I'm exaggerating or making this up. It's all there in black and white.

Moreover, there were witnesses to the whole ordeal, so it's not like I'm making it up. I still have the tumor to this day. I'm hesitant to get it removed because the procedure involves going through my nose with a tube, and there's a risk of complications. If they accidentally touch something other than the tumor, I could end up with severe brain damage. That's a terrifying prospect, and it's why I've chosen to live with the tumor instead of risking a potentially worse outcome. I'm scared of making things worse.

If I talk about the chest compression procedure, you're unconscious and don't feel anything. But afterward, you're left feeling like your ribs are bruised or broken—it's a really uncomfortable sensation. But I've learned to cope with it, though. On top of the physical pain, I also deal with bipolar disorder and depression, which can be overwhelming at times. However, I've found that my pain medication helps alleviate some of those symptoms as well.

If I were to take other medications, like antidepressants or mood stabilizers, they might help with my mental health. But now, when it comes to psychiatric medications for my mental health, I feel like they're worse than pain medications. I don't like feeling sedated, lethargic, or zombie-like.

The pain medication, on the other hand, makes me feel normal and motivated to do things. With the psychiatric medications, I feel like I'm not living a normal life. And you know, people often judge you when you go to the hospital, thinking you're just seeking narcotics or something. But if they understood my situation, they'd realize that the psychiatric medications are actually more dangerous than the pain medications. Those medications can put you to sleep, just like heroin does. They're downers, and that's not what I need. And on top of that, there are multiple side effects from those medicines. I've been struggling with all this since my car accident. You go to the hospital, and suddenly, there's a whole administrative process involved, from doctor to patient. It's like, the doctor wants to do their job, but the administration gets in the way. It's weird and messed up. But what they don't understand is that people are dying from fentanyl and other drugs, whether they're from France, Mexico, or for recreational use on the streets. And we're the ones who get the short end of the stick in the US. We're the ones who really need these medications to live a normal life.

However, hospital administrations are more concerned with making money. They're prioritizing profits over patient care. Doctors, on the other hand, have an oath to save every patient, and they have good intentions. But the administration is holding them back—dictating what they can and can't do. And yet, they still bill Medicare and Medicaid for services that aren't even helpful. It's frustrating, and I get upset when I see doctors being restricted from doing their jobs properly. They should be able to practice medicine without administrative interference.

All of this keeps me frustrated and upset. These doctors are supposed to be professionals, but they're not doing their job properly. It's like they're waiting for you to worsen before they'll actually do something. Like last night, my mom went to the hospital, and the doctor—I think the hospital director or someone high up—sent her home with nothing. It's like they're more concerned with protecting themselves from liability than actually helping patients. They sent my mom home with nothing—no pain management, no treatment, no help. She told them she didn't have a pain management doctor anymore because he was retiring, but they just dismissed her. It's like they want her to come back so they can charge her again. I see a little bit of politics and racism going on here. It's hidden, but it's there. It's in the way they're dividing people and ignoring their needs. I have proof of my injury, but they're not taking it seriously. It's like they're more concerned with protecting themselves than actually helping patients. It's frustrating and upsetting.

Coming back to my pain, I've had three surgeries and three reconstructive procedures on my body. All they can say is that it's nothing and that it's just a minor issue. But they don't understand the struggle I'm going through. Without medication, I don't feel like doing anything because I'm in so much pain. I can't cook, wash clothes, or even go to the store without getting tired and feeling pain in my back and feet. I limp more without the medication. It's like they don't understand that my medication is what allows me to function at 90% capacity, whereas without it, I'm only at 50%. It's a real mess what they're doing to people like me who are genuinely injured and in need of help instead of just assuming we're recreational drug users, which is absolutely not fair.

Chapter 11: The Aftermath

After being discharged from the hospital and completing my rehabilitation, I wanted legal advice. I consulted a lawyer who agreed to take on my case. During our discussions, we discovered I had insurance coverage on the car involved in the incident, which I wasn't oblivious to. Thankfully, we received the maximum payout of $30,000 from the insurance company. However, just as I thought I would finally receive some financial relief, Medicare stepped in and put a hold on the check. Once again, I was left without any funds.

The lawyer then suggested that we consider suing the property owners due to the insufficient lighting and other hazardous conditions that contributed to the incident. He guaranteed that we had a strong case and could receive significant money. At first, I was hesitant to pursue this route because I was worried that the property owners would strike back by throwing me out of my home.

Despite my reservations, the lawyer remained optimistic and encouraged us to proceed with the lawsuit. He even offered to provide us with monthly support to guarantee that we wouldn't lose our home during the legal process. He told us that there was a lot of money at stake and that he would do everything he could to protect our interests. After careful consideration, we decided to proceed with the lawsuit, hoping for a favorable outcome. I'm still trying to process my experience with my lawyer. It's unbelievable how they took advantage of me. I could trust him, but, in the end, he didn't do his job. It was like he was working against me. I remember my former employer warning me about lawyers. He said that they're like a pit of snakes. I didn't believe him at the time, but now I realize he was right.

When it came time to settle and go through the deposition, my lawyer was barely paying attention—he was almost asleep. When they mentioned my brother's name, his lawyer wasn't even present, and he didn't contest anything. I felt like I'd been robbed. I'll never trust a lawyer again. I thought I could rely on him to help me, but he failed me miserably. It's a hard lesson to learn.

Now, I'm dealing with my family situation. My mom depends on me a lot, and I'm trying to take care of her. If I talk about my brother, well, he's just a different story. He's been in and out of rehab several times, and it's always the same pattern. He goes in and says he will change, but never listens and ends up back where he started.

The last time was the worst. He went to a rehab center near where I grew up, and he told me they hit him and gave him shots to sedate him. I couldn't believe it. That's not rehab; that's abuse. He said it happened for the first two days he was there. I don't know what to do anymore. I've tried to help him many times, but he never gets better.

I'm still trying to process the horrific experiences my brother went through at that so-called Christian rehab center. He told me they gave him vitamins to help with his addiction, supposedly, but it was all a lie. The third time he was there, he said there were older ladies—around 50 or 55 years old—who were also being 'treated.' But what really shocked me was when he said the owner, who claimed to be a Christian, would tell the staff to shut the ladies up or make them behave, and then they'd slap them around. It's disgusting.

I confronted them about their actions, saying, 'You can't call yourselves Christians if you're going to beat people up and slap them around!' But they just kept saying, 'God bless you,' and pretending to be something they're not. My brother was right when he said the association took place. They charged us excessive money to keep him there, and when we tried to take him out, they raised the price even more. It was like they thought we were made of money.

To make matters worse, the cartel is involved in human trafficking. They were charging people to cross the river and trying to crush those who couldn't pay. I lost a lot of money trying to help my brother, and he even tried to cross the river once but didn't make it. That's when I told him he needed to seek asylum, given all the proof we had of the cartel's involvement. He even showed me a picture of a newspaper article about three kids who were poisoned with cake—the same cake they were giving him at the rehab center. It's just terrible. It's like they had a commissary or canteen system, but instead of using it to buy things, they were poisoning people.

We've been trying to help him, but he's not making it easy. He's always asking for money every day. We've sent him money before, but he doesn't listen. He's stubborn and only cares about getting more money. I'm worried he's going to hurt my mom one of these days. She's already in the hospital with COVID again, and now Johnny's mom has pneumonia because of the hurricane. It feels like everything is falling apart. Despite all my challenges, I'm trying to stay positive and focus on the good. I believe that God has a purpose for me, and maybe that purpose is to help others who are going through similar struggles. I've always been humble, and my experiences have taught me to care deeply about others. I've been in tough situations and know how hard it can be. So, I'm hoping my story can inspire and help others somehow. I hope everything turns around soon and I can start seeing positive changes in my life.

I remember that the person asking for money wanted us to wire it to their bank account. They claimed that in exchange, they would pick up my brother, take him to a safe house, and then provide proof that he was okay. They also said they would get him papers to protect him from the cartel and border authorities.

But I'm starting to think it was all just a scam. The more I learn, the more I realize that the cartel is involved in everything. They're even using propaganda to control people's minds. I just got in touch with a lady who was helping my brother, and she connected me to a guy named Armando. He gave me a number to which to wire the money, but I'm not sure if it was a good idea. Well, now I'm just trying to stay focused and get through this difficult time. My mom is still in the hospital, and I'm worried about her. I'm also concerned about my brother and what might happen to him. I just want to get him to safety and make sure he's okay. I had a video that showed the route we needed to take, and I passed it along to the people who were supposed to help my brother. They told me they would take him to a motel, and everything would be fine. I believed them, but things didn't go as planned. When it was time to meet the guy who was supposed to take my brother to safety, he had a flat tire or some other excuse. He told me to go to a restaurant on the other side of the river, saying it would be easy. But when we got there, we were met with a border patrol checkpoint on a hill overlooking the river. I couldn't believe it, as he had never warned me about this.

It was like they had made it sound so simple, saying they had done it before and there would be no problem. But they got scared and backed out when it came down to it. I lost the money I had paid for them, and it was all for nothing. It's frustrating because they could have tried again and again until they succeeded, but instead, they just gave up.

I think these people use bait to trap others in their scams. If someone else pays more money to cross the border, they'll prioritize that person and find a way to get them across. It's all about the money. They're crooked and will do whatever it takes to get what they want.

've fallen victim to a devastating scam. I paid a woman $700, trusting she'd help my brother cross the border safely, promising to get him an ID and ensure everything went smoothly. But it was all a deceitful lie. She vanished with my money, leaving me with a useless phone number. I'm torn about reporting her, fearing it could put my brother in jeopardy. To make matters worse, she's still trying to trick me, claiming she can't find the person who was supposed to assist my brother. I'm left feeling frustrated, helpless, and wary of seeking help.

I'm so frustrated because I know this woman is just giving me the runaround. She took my money and didn't deliver on her promises. It's hard to be cautious and avoid getting scammed again when you're desperate to help your loved ones. It's heartbreaking to deal with so many dishonest people who take advantage of our desperation to reunite with our loved ones. My brother is one of them; he's always blaming my mom for his situation, but he's had opportunities to fix it and hasn't taken them. What's even more complicated is that he was born in the US, but my mom was deported while pregnant with him, so he grew up in another country. To make matters worse, he's been deported multiple times himself but still doesn't listen and make changes. It's like he's not taking responsibility for his life, and it's hard to watch.

Now, he's stuck and needs to find a way to return home, maybe through asylum. I'm trying to help him, but it's hard when he's not taking responsibility for his actions. We regularly pay him around $1000-$2000 and pay his rent. He's 40-something years old, so he should be able to care for himself, but he's not. Despite what I might have mentioned earlier, he's not in a relationship or married. It's just him, and he's relying on us to support him financially. I'm trying to stay patient and help him, but it's frustrating when he doesn't try to improve his situation.

My brother has a daughter in the U.S., and she wants him to be with her. But I've never met him, and I'm not even sure if I want to. Only my mom knows him well. I take care of her, and we meet regularly. My sister is also here in the U.S., but my brother is the only one still in Mexico. Our story could be interesting to many people, especially immigrants from Mexico and other Hispanic communities. My brother speaks English well, has attended school, and earned his G.E.D. here.

Chapter 12: My Mother

My mother's health issues began when she was pregnant with my third or fourth brother. She was receiving care at a clinic for the poor, run by nuns, near a Guadalupe church. Unfortunately, my father, a carpenter, was unreliable and struggled with addiction, leaving my mother to fend for herself. After giving birth, she had to walk to find money to pay for her care, which marked the beginning of her decline. She eventually fell, broke her hip, and required a replacement.

As the eldest child, I've taken on a significant caregiving role, especially since my brother moved to Mexico. I've been caring for my mother for as long as I can remember, but now I have the added responsibility of supporting my brother from a distance. Despite the challenges, I recognized the blessings of caring for my mother.

Our relationship is intricate since I often get upset with her because she doesn't listen to my advice, but I never scream at her. My mother is now 74 years old, and I'm 58. She had me when she was just 16 and married at 15 or 16. As the firstborn, I've always felt a deep sense of responsibility toward her.

My mother's longevity is proof of her good genes, which were inherited from her parents of Indian descent from Mexico. My grandmother used to share traditional remedies with me, such as using the avocado pit to aid digestion. She'd cook, crush, and mix it with lard to help with constipation. I remember finding it unpleasant, but it worked. Despite our imperfections and human nature, I've learned to prioritize caring for my loved ones, including my mother. We've had our share of conflicts, particularly when she struggled to accept my sexuality. She would sometimes react harshly, even threatening to kick me out of the house, but I've chosen to put aside our differences and continue caring for her.

It's essential to acknowledge that nobody is perfect, and we all have our flaws. However, it's crucial to prioritize love, care, and acceptance, especially toward our close ones. My mother's acceptance of my sexuality was challenging, especially when my brother started having children, and I became more open about my identity. However, my priority remains caring for her. I've held onto my faith since I was around seven or eight years old, when I was introduced to God and Jesus through gospel songs and tent revivals in Mexico. I believe the devil tried to distance me from my faith, and my struggles with paint sniffing led to a tumor and damaged my vocal cords.

Despite this, I still enjoy singing and playing the piano, even though my voice is no longer smooth and I struggle to hit the right notes. I attribute this to paint sniffing, which I believe affected my vocal cords. Nevertheless, my love for music and faith persisted.

Anyhow, my mother's passing was a devastating loss for our family. The pain and grief we felt were endless. Her absence left a void in our lives that could never be filled.

Reflecting on these experiences, I've come to appreciate the complexities of human relationships and the enduring power of family bonds. Even in the face of adversity, the love and support of family can provide comfort and strength.

When I think of my past, I've come to realize that the traumatic experiences I've faced, including being molested, are part of a larger family curse. My godfather, who abused me, has sons who have also committed similar acts, perpetuating a cycle of harm. I've learned through my pastor that this chain of abuse can only be broken through forgiveness and the power of Jesus' blood. I've seen this pattern repeat itself in families struggling with addiction, where the cycle continues until someone seeks spiritual rebirth. Unfortunately, I've lived through this reality, and it has affected my desire to have children. However, I've found joy in raising my adopted nephew, Christopher, who has given me a sense of fatherhood. I'm grateful for this opportunity and feel blessed to have experienced the love and responsibility that come with it.

Although I've always known I was gay, I did date girls in the past. They would show interest in me by sending me letters and asking me to dance. I had girlfriends, but it never worked out because I didn't feel the same way. I kissed them, but that's as far as it went. I was never attracted to them, but I didn't know how to express that.

Looking back, I realized I was trying to fit societal norms. Despite this, I don't regret my experiences because they led me to where I am today. I believe God made me perfect, and my life's journey, including meeting my partner John at church, was part of His plan. I'm at peace with my identity and grateful for the path that brought me here.

I've struggled with the idea of God accepting me for who I am, but I found comfort in a scripture that says,

"I will forgive whomever I choose to forgive, and I will have mercy on whomever I show mercy"
(Romans 9:15–16).

My pastor agreed that this verse suggests God's mercy and forgiveness are not limited by human standards. I realized I'm not bad, as I don't hurt anyone and help those in need. I see that everyone, regardless of their sexual orientation or marital status, commits sins. Even married couples go beyond reproduction in their intimate relationships. I understand that we're all sinners, and Jesus came for us and not for the perfect. I'm content with my way of life and find comfort in my faith. I'll continue praying to be with God one day. I'm astonished when people deny the existence of God by considering the intricate design of the universe. The stars, sun, and Earth's precise axis suggest a creator. I believe a higher power puts everything in order, and it's working perfectly. I'm surprised when people, even college students, argue against God's existence without knowing scripture.

They try to understand through their own wisdom, not God's. That's why I pray for God's wisdom, asking Him to show me the meaning of things, not relying on my own understanding. I don't trust my own wisdom; I trust God, who created the universe. My pastor taught me to pray this way, and I've experienced moments where the Holy Spirit has given me understanding. It's an incredible feeling.

I understand what he's saying now. I've seen people like Scientologists and scientists question God's existence. They ask questions like, "Why did Jesus pray to the Father if he's God?" But they don't understand that Jesus was in human form, just like us. He wasn't in his full divine power. God is omnipotent and can be everywhere at once.

That's why Jesus asked the Father for forgiveness on the cross. He had the Holy Spirit in him, but he was still flesh. They don't understand this, and I think the devil is deceiving them, just like he did with Judas. Jesus gave Judas the bread, knowing he would betray him to fulfill the prophecy. Even God had to allow this for our sake. I see how God works, and it's amazing. I remember when Jesus gave the bread to Judas, and he got up to buy food for the feast. But the devil had already deceived Judas, and he betrayed Jesus for money. When Mary washed Jesus' feet with expensive oil, Judas questioned it, but Jesus said, 'You will always have the poor, but you won't always have me.' Money is nothing compared to spiritual things. I see it now.

I thank God for showing me His wisdom. I want my readers to understand that without Him, we can't do anything. I'm still alive despite seven near-death experiences and ongoing attacks from the enemy. They want to harm me because I serve the Lord and spread His message. The devil wants to take as many souls as possible before judgment day.

I've seen famous stars like Kurt Cobain, Amy Winehouse, and Jim Morrison die young despite their wealth and power. They lost their souls because they didn't follow God's ways. We don't have to be perfect, but we must admit our sinfulness and the fact that we'll be judged one day. Many people don't grasp this reality, thinking they'll just die and that's it. But our souls will go somewhere, and it'll be too late to change.

I hope my book helps people understand this. I'm not perfect, but I try not to sin, and the Holy Spirit convicts me when I do. I know this because I feel bad, and I ask for forgiveness. The difference between Christians and others is that we're forgiven, not perfect. We need to accept our mistakes and those of others and forgive them.

The Bible says that if we don't forgive, God won't forgive us. It may sound harsh, but there's also happiness and peace in following God's ways. When I give to others, I feel greater joy than when I receive. Even when I give to someone on the street, I don't worry where the money goes; I just know it's a good deed. If someone chooses to buy beer or cigarettes with the money I give them, that's not my concern; I've done my part in helping them.

However, if I see someone struggling with addiction, I'll offer them coffee or food instead. I know the difference and trust the Holy Spirit to guide me. I've been in tough situations before and am grateful to be out of them. Now, I see my brother struggling, and I constantly encourage him to search for help through church and a pastor. I believe that's the only way to overcome struggles. Without God, we're nothing—zero. I don't get tired of telling them this because I care about their well-being.

Chapter 13: Today and Tomorrow

My relationship with Johnny and his mother was complicated from the start. When I first met Johnny, his mom and sister clarified that they disapproved of me. They often said hurtful things to us, and I sensed deep-seated jealousy. I believe she felt left out when I entered Johnny's life, even though we tried to include her in our activities and spend quality time with her.

Despite her behavior, I was determined to show respect, having been taught by my grandparents never to disrespect my elders. However, her mean-spirited comments and actions made it challenging for me to navigate this delicate family dynamic. Looking back, I realize that this situation taught me valuable lessons about resilience, empathy, and understanding.

Johnny's mom would often criticize my mother, who wasn't even involved in our lives. It was strange, and I began to realize that she might have had emotional struggles. Despite her behavior, Johnny and I made a pact not to let her negativity come between us. We've been dealing with this dynamic for 20 years, but everything changed when she passed away almost a month ago. Her absence has left a void, and I miss her presence, even with all her quirks. She often forgot things and needed constant reminders, but Johnny wanted to take care of her at home. She refused to consider professional help, despite my concerns. Looking back, I understand that he wanted to keep her close, but I worry that his decision might have been driven by a desire to hold on to the past. I've learned to accept that people can make their own choices, even if I disagree with them. In Johnny's mom's case, I felt she wasn't taking responsibility for her own life and sensed that something was bound to go wrong. Unfortunately, my fears were realized when she passed away. I don't like to dwell on negative emotions or drama, and I've learned to walk away from situations that become too much.

Johnny's mother, while well-intentioned, was unfortunately influenced by her daughter's negative feelings towards me. Despite our efforts to help her—her daughter's hatred towards me blinded her to the good we were trying to do. Her daughter's hatred was a constant source of tension between us and Johnny's mother. It created a rift within our family, tearing us apart. Despite our love and affection for her, we could not bridge the gap created by her daughter's influence.

My mother-in-law's passing was a devastating loss for our family. We missed her dearly, even though her presence could sometimes be challenging due to her dementia. Her confusion and forgetfulness often led to misunderstandings and frustrations. Despite her flaws, my mother-in-law was a part of our family, and her absence left a void in our lives. Her passing reminded me of the importance of cherishing our loved ones, even when they are imperfect. I believe that with a little more understanding and compassion, we could have overcome the challenges posed by my mother-in-law's daughter. However, the deep-seated hatred between them proved to be an insurmountable obstacle. In the past, I've even turned to substance abuse as a coping mechanism, but I've since found comfort in my faith and my relationship with Johnny. I've been praying for guidance and peace, but it's clear that some things are outside my control. I've come to accept that Johnny's mom is gone, and I'm focusing on moving forward.

On a separate note, I want to share my passion for Israel, which I believe is a sacred place. My connection to Israel is deeply personal and rooted in my faith. I feel a strong empathy for the land and its people, and I hope to explore this aspect of my life further. I'm grateful for the United States' support of Israel, as I believe it's a crucial alliance. According to the Bible, many nations will oppose Israel, but I take comfort in knowing that God will ultimately protect His people. I've always been fascinated by the Jewish faith, and I've recently been exploring documentaries about Judaism.

However, I struggle to understand why many Jews don't recognize Jesus as the Messiah. It's striking to me that Jesus, the King of the Jews, was born into the Jewish faith, yet many Jews don't accept Him as their savior. I recall watching a documentary where a group was preaching about Jesus in a Jewish community, and they were met with resistance. One woman, in particular, seemed consumed by anger and hostility, which I can only attribute to spiritual blindness. It's heartbreaking to see people reject the truth, but I trust in God's plan and the fulfillment of biblical prophecy.

As the Bible says,

The devil can blind people's eyes to the truth, but I pray for understanding and revelation.

I've always been fascinated by Jesus' statement, 'I am the truth,' yet many people, including the Jews, didn't recognize Him as the Messiah. Despite performing numerous miracles, He couldn't convince them of His divinity. This reminds me of modern-day Christians who preach without seeking God's wisdom. I recall a recent experience where someone preached without being adequately prepared, and it struck me as lacking in spiritual authority.

A pastor once taught me that to spread God's word effectively, one must be blessed and walk in righteousness. This means being holy and pure, not just for a moment but in a consistent state. Fasting and seeking God's cleansing can help achieve this, but it's not the same as being holy like Jesus, who was God incarnate. I've learned that preaching God's word requires more than just belief. It demands a deep connection with the Holy Spirit and a commitment to living a sanctified life. Otherwise, our words can fall flat, lacking the power and conviction that come from being a vessel for God's truth. From that moment on, I devoted myself to learning music, inspired by the teacher who had introduced me to the piano. I was amazed at how quickly I picked up songs like 'Chariots of Fire' and 'The Pink Panther.' Music brought me comfort and solace, especially during difficult times. The teacher's mom, who had passed away, would often remind me that 'God is still on His throne.' This phrase became a source of strength for me, a reminder that God is always present, even in struggles. Her belief in me and her conviction that we would meet again in heaven gave me the courage to face my challenges.

One of the most significant experiences that helped me confront my demons was when I felt Jesus' presence in the prayer room. It was an unforgettable moment, and I knew that He was with me. This experience gave me the strength to overcome my struggles, including the pain of my brother's mistakes. He had gotten caught up in drugs and taken the blame for something he shouldn't have done.

Despite his youth and inexperience, he faced severe consequences. But through it all, I knew that God was still in control, and that gave me the courage to keep moving forward. My brother's struggles with addiction and anger issues led to a cycle of incarceration, deportation, and relapse. Despite my family's efforts to help him, including my half-sister and father figure in Mexico, he refused to listen. Eventually, he ended up in Reynosa, where a friend of his, a lady, tried to assist him. However, my mom insisted on sending him money directly, which he would use for drugs. I tried to intervene by sending the money to the lady instead, but my mom's stubbornness and my brother's manipulation prevented it. After two failed attempts at rehab, I insisted on finding a Christian rehab that taught the Bible.

However, despite claiming to be a Christian, the owner had a disturbing approach. He would instruct the staff to abuse the female patients, including 15-year-old girls, physically to "make them behave." This was not only un-Christian but also inhumane. I later discovered that this rehab was likely run by the cartel, which explained the owner's knowledge of various colonies and cultures. This experience was a harsh reminder of the darkness that can masquerade as help and the importance of finding genuine support.

I've realized that some areas are divided into territories controlled by various groups, making it difficult to intervene. Despite our efforts, we've reached a point where we can't do anything more to help my brother. I've advised him to seek asylum, as he has evidence of the cartel's threats and violence against him.

Final Reflection

I'm doing well now and staying on the right path, and I want to encourage anyone out there who might be going through a tough time. I've faced my own battles—whether it was addiction, trauma, or moments where I felt completely lost and overwhelmed.

But through it all, I've learned something important: holding on to hope and having faith in God can make all the difference.

I know what it's like to feel like you're at the end of your rope, to feel like things will never get better. But I'm here to tell you that no matter how bad things may seem, your story isn't over. God has a plan for each of us, even when we can't see it.

Sometimes, the darkest moments are the ones that shape us the most, pushing us to grow, to change, and to reach out for the support we need.

If you're struggling—whether it's with addiction, trauma, or just feeling like you're stuck in a cycle you can't break—don't give up.

There is always a way forward, even if it's just one small step at a time. Keep fighting, keep believing, and surround yourself with people who lift you up and remind you of your worth. Life has its ups and downs, but remember that you're not alone.

There is hope and healing on the other side of whatever you're facing. Don't let the lies of hopelessness convince you that you're not worth it or that things will never change. They will. Trust in God's timing, trust in His love for you, and keep moving forward. Your life has a purpose, and there are better days ahead.

The Pastor and His Wife

Me Alongside My Grandfather

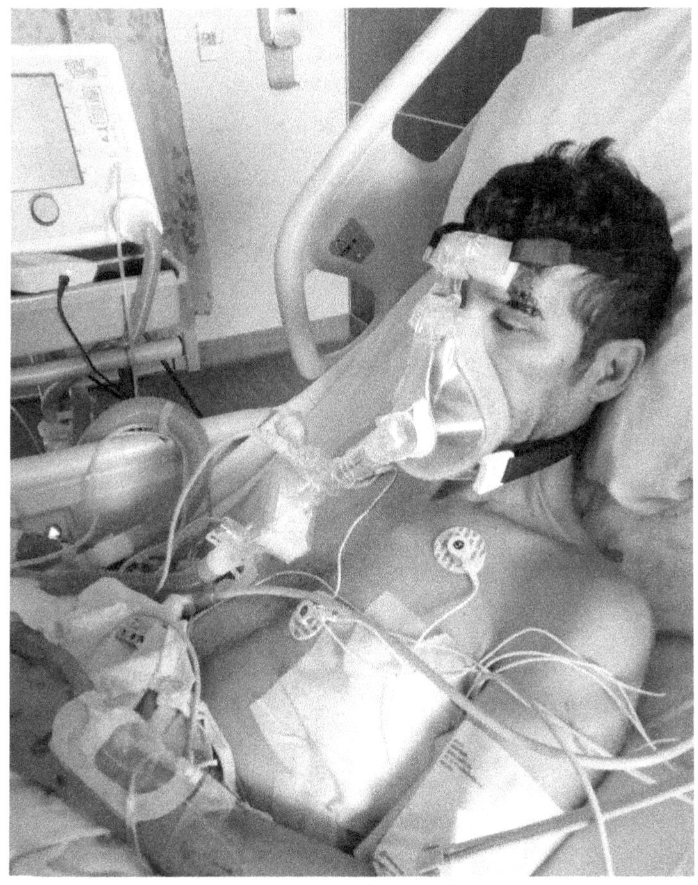

Me During The Accident